The Meandering Way

The
Meandering
Way

Leading by Following the Spirit

Gary A. Shockley

THE
ALBAN
INSTITUTE

Herndon, Virginia
www.alban.org

The Alban Institute
2121 Cooperative Way, Suite 100
Herndon, VA 20171

Scripture quotations, unless otherwise noted, are from the New Revised Standard Version of the Bible, © 1989, Division of Christian Education of the National Council of Churches of Christ in the United States of America, and are used by permission.

Cover design by Wendy Ronga, Hampton Design Group.

Library of Congress Cataloging-in-Publication Data

Shockley, Gary A.
    The meandering way : leading by following the spirit / Gary A. Shockley.
        p. cm.
    Includes bibliographical references.
    ISBN 978-1-56699-342-5
    1. Christian leadership. 2. Holy Spirit. I. Title.

    BV652.1.S56 2007
    248.4--dc22

                                    2007013391

    12   11   10   09   08   07   UG   1   2   3   4   5   6

To my parents, Richard and Alice, my first spiritual
guides, with love and gratitude.

Contents

Foreword

This is a book that meanders. Now, normally that might seem like a bad thing, as a critique suggesting that the book has no compelling point. Yet in this case, saying that it meanders is high praise. Gary Shockley has written a book that not only describes a way of being and of leading, but he has written it in a manner that draws you into the experience of meandering. This book meanders, and through it Gary welcomes you to a way that living life as it should be lived, to a way of leading people as they should be led. Unfortunately, too few pastors and other leaders are willing to meander. Instead, they live life in a driven way, and that's why they struggle.

There's no question that we live in a hectic, frenzied world. Most of us feel set upon by the gods of hurry, gods who command that we rush from one commitment to another in order to appease them. As we rush to appease these faceless, nameless gods, we end up sacrificing our health and our lives. The reality is that these gods can never be appeased because they don't exist. So what are we really serving? It certainly isn't God.

Church leaders are not immune to the beckoning call of these gods. Many pastors and lay leaders serve these gods of hurry rather than God. Why? Because these false gods shout while God whispers, and we are attracted to the noise. As a result, too many of us lead in a way that the world deems successful, but not in a way that God would consider successful. We try to lead *in place of* God, rather than as partners *with* God. It is in the midst of this question of whom we serve that the genius of the "meandering way" becomes apparent. Gary gives a name to a whole different approach, a way of leadership that is rooted in wandering *with* God as we discover what God can make possible.

By showing us how to meander with God, Gary Shockley reveals the way into wisdom. This book is filled with wisdom that only comes when as leaders we are willing to wander in wonder with God. What are some of the wisdoms Gary's work reveals? They are pearls of wisdom that, if polished in our own leadership, will allow us to lead our congregations with grace, love, wisdom, and light. And the wisdom Gary shares with us comes straight out of his experiences, some of which might have caused us to feel humiliated, but in Gary's life led him to become humble. Drawing on his own experiences as the pastor of small churches in a yoked pastorate, as an associate pastor in a large church, as new church development pastor, as a fundraising consultant, and as pastor of a larger church, Gary delves deeply into his experiences to reveal how God leads us to face ourselves honestly so that we can get out of the way and instead learn to truly lead *with* God.

Let me give you some examples of what I mean. Using himself as a case study, Gary shows us how easy it is for us to become driven to accomplish success for God, rather than being led by God to do God's will. He also shows how, in the process, what we do often lacks success because it is focused on us rather than on God. He demonstrates how easy it is for us to promote our own achievements and ourselves rather than what God is doing in our midst.

In the process of exploring how our "success-driven" demons sidetrack us, he offers us a new path-a path that leads to a greater awareness of where God is in our lives. For example, he reminds us that God led the Israelites to wander in the desert for 40 years so that they could learn to trust and follow God no matter which direction they went. In the same way, he reminds us that God calls us to wander in a way that allows us to discover and follow God's markers and to become transformed through our following. He reminds us that instead of driving ourselves and others toward a goal, we can learn much by taking side trips off the well-trod path-trips that lead us to discover wonders and beauty. And when we lead congregations to take these side trips, we invite them to discover undiscovered territory where God's beauty is really apparent.

He reminds us of how much we need to move to that place where the time we spend truly reflects what we most deeply value in life, rather than wasting time appeasing those false idols that forcefully drive us to...to...where? He reminds us that we shouldn't be wasting time trying to figure out what the *right* path is. Instead, all we are called to do is to walk with God wherever God leads, and to trust that whatever path we are on is God's path. In the end, meandering isn't just about wandering with God; it is about the relationship we form with God when we are willing to trust God.

This book, and Gary himself, is a reflection of a new style of leadership that is emerging in the mainline church. It is a leadership approach that cares less about the church as an organization and an institution and much more about the church as a community of people following God wherever God will lead. It is an approach that cares much more about leading people to experience God directly in their lives than it is about maintaining the status quo or tradition. It's an approach that I share and that connects Gary and me, that has connected us ever since we studied spirituality together as part of a doctoral program at Duquesne University in the early 1990s. We have shared a passion for creating congregations that are more focused on following where God is leading rather than focusing on where the church has been. And this book is a reflection of that passion.

There is so much wisdom for leaders in these pages, if we are willing to meander with Gary Shockley as he teaches us how to wander with God. In a world in which people feel the constant need to rush, hurry, achieve, accomplish, do, and get somewhere fast, we are reminded that there is a way of leading that imitates Moses and Jesus: meandering with a purpose.

This is a book that gently meanders, and as it does, it teaches us to lead with a much wiser spirit.

N. Graham Standish

Acknowlegments

When my wife Kim and I were dating I splurged one evening and made reservations at Alfred's Victorian—a quaint, somewhat highbrow restaurant, in Middletown, Pennsylvania. Even though she was already madly in love with me, I felt that continuing to make a good impression on Kim would pay me greater dividends later.

I don't remember what Kim was wearing, but I am sure she looked great—she always does. I do, however, remember my attire, right down to the blue polyester sport coat with the wide lapel purchased at Kmart. It framed my smart blue and white checkered, short-sleeved shirt, set off by an extra-wide navy blue tie. How she kept her hands off me during dinner, I will never know.

I remember this event well because we ended up sitting adjacent to a group of eight to ten well-dressed professional men who looked like they actually belonged in a place like Alfred's. Short, well-spoken toasts, punctuated by the clinking glasses of champagne, drifted over to our table. Something about partnerships, a law firm, the publishing of a book. Eventually copies of said book appeared from under their table and were joyously passed around with more toasts and offers of congratulations. We felt terribly out of place.

Kim and I were in our first year of college. I was already serving an inner-city church in downtown Harrisburg, Pennsylvania, and Kim was working as a sweeperette at nearby Hershey Park. Not to be outdone by a bunch of "suits," we toasted each other with our tap water. The glasses made a thud that just couldn't compete with the jocularity of our neighbors. We had a great time together anyway, though, because we were in love.

I remember thinking then how wonderful it would be to write a book and how great it would be to have my closest friends lifting their glasses in celebration with me. But from that vantage point it seemed like a ridiculous wish. By the time you read this book, however, my celebration party will have happened. I hope to take Kim back to Alfred's to do it up right this time.

As I lift my glass, I will express gratitude to many people who helped make me and this project a reality. I will thank my parents, Richard and Alice Shockley, for their love and belief in me. My in-laws, Ed and Barb Shultz, who taught me how to see life in a new way. My brother, Rick, who has become my playmate again—only this time in middle age. For my sisters, Carol and Alison, who have had to live under the shadow of their pastor brother and put up with his table graces that went on far too long. For my grandparents, aunts, uncles, and cousins who remind me of my roots. For all the friends over the years who journeyed with me if only for a season. Especially to Bob for the early flying and sailing lessons. For every person who suffered under my early sermons and looked as though they were listening. For Lisa McCauley, who helped guide me through a difficult valley and to learn to more fully experience God's presence there. For the churches I have been blessed to serve—Riverside, Austin, Costello, Keating Summit, Red Haw, Graysville, Nebo, Ingomar, Cornerstone, and now St. Luke's and HopeSpring. For my friends and colleagues in ministry—especially Paul, who died before this book was published and is now viewing my journey from a vastly different perspective.

I especially thank my sons, Aaron and Jake, whom I love and in whom I can see the better parts of myself and God. And my wife, Kim, who continues to be the love of my life, my very best friend, and the anchor that keeps me steady. Someday I want to grow up to be just like her—without the dress.

My gratitude to the people of the Alban Institute and especially my editor, Beth Gaede, who has been an encouraging and patient guide in this journey and to Andrea Lee who helped polish this work.

Maybe I could have gone a long way in this journey without the help of some of the people I have mentioned—but I am sure glad I didn't!

Introduction

Sailing in the Desert

I was born and raised near the Delaware Bay in a small fishing village called Lewes Beach. This was where my father and his family grew up. He and his only brother lived with my grandparents in a converted Pullman car my grandfather bought in 1929 for 50 dollars.

I remember stories my father would tell about how he helped my grandfather in his charter-boat fishing business, how he went high diving off the mast of tall sailing ships in the channel, and the hours he spent by the bay surf fishing with rods he and his father had crafted by hand.

As a child, I spent as much time as my father could tolerate standing close enough to hear the drag on his reel or his muttered incantations over a worm, spinner, or popper, hoping to lure a fish to his hook. Something about needing to be near the water as often as possible was passed on from my grandfather to my father and then to me. These days I am never more relaxed and fulfilled than when I am near the water. Sunning on the beach, fly-fishing in a cold mountain stream, or simply relaxing by a pond, I manage to discover the better part of me. This wasn't always the case though.

As a very young child I was deathly afraid of the water. I kept this fear mostly to myself, although I used to have nightmares about people I loved drowning at sea. Hearing reports of occasional drownings off nearby Rehoboth Beach only worsened my fears. The undertow in the ocean can be a silent, deadly foe. It seemed each summer some unsuspecting tourist went into the surf too far and never came back. Not me! I never went in deeper than my knees.

My earliest fears found substance when I had a near-drowning experience at a place called Trap Pond. I was six years old and my parents signed my sister and me up for swimming lessons. I was following instructions, as best I could, when I dove, or rather flopped, headfirst off a box just beneath the pond's surface and landed face first in the waist-deep water. I was then supposed to point my arms straight out in front of me like an arrow and kick my feet like crazy. Instead, I hit the water so that it filled my nose and in a panic I gasped for air. Not a particularly smart thing to do when you are underwater. I flailed in the cool liquid atmosphere like a newborn eaglet tossed from its nest. My feet kicked all the more forcefully, driving me deeper into the abyss. All my childhood fears of drowning were suddenly coming true. And then an arm reached down to pluck me from my watery grave. The hand grabbed me by my shorts and hoisted me back to the surface where I kept right on kicking and hitting air. I was not so gently plopped down on the sand. Red-faced and exhausted from the experience I made a promise to God. The first of many. I would never go into the water again. Near it, around it, and maybe even above it, but never *in* it again!

I kept that promise until I was 13 when I taught myself how to swim in a neighbor's pool. To this day I still prefer the shallow end of the pool. And if I am unfortunate enough to drift on my inflatable raft over to the deep end of the pool by means of current or conniving, I find myself getting tense and red faced all over again.

Twenty-some years later, in my early thirties, I was invited to go sailing. My best friend, Bob, whom I always admired as fearless and strong and never tense or red faced about anything, invited me to join him in a weekend of sailing on the river. I worked through my usual list of excuses as to why I wouldn't be able to join him, but Bob saw through each transparent lie. He knew all about my fear of the water and eventually convinced me that it would be okay. Bob and his wife Tammy met my wife and me at the river. It was a beautiful fall day. Bright, blue sky. Puffy marshmallow clouds. Calm, tranquil waters. And just enough breeze to carry us out to sea.

Did I mention that Bob is fearless? Bob is the same friend who took flying lessons when we were in high school. Once he developed his competencies and was cleared to fly with passengers, we would take his borrowed Cessna and cruise the air like teens today cruise the local strip. It was Bob who gave me my first flying lesson. It was Bob who showed me how much physical strength I really had in my fingers as I gripped the seat beneath me, hanging on for dear life as he practiced dives, stalls, and other scary maneuvers. I managed to survive Bob's flying. Now I would see about his sailing.

Bob gave us some quick sailing instructions, pointing out things like masts and jibs and tillers and such. With a hoist of the main sail we were on our way. Not far from shore the boat listed to one side as the sail caught wind and began to glide across the water. I could feel my childhood fear of the water welling inside me. I tried to hide it even though I am sure my reddened face was giving me away.

Bob walked around the deck of the boat as though his feet had suction cups on the bottom, keeping him steady and sure-footed. I sat next to my wife at the back of the boat, once again testing my finger strength on the seat beneath me. Noticing my rigid posture, Bob reassured me, "It is virtually impossible to tip this kind of sailboat." "Virtually" being the operative word here, I thought. "It has a keel under the hull that allows the boat to practically sail on its side," he explained. Great consolation.

We were well underway, the shoreline shrinking to a mere hairline crack on the horizon. Bob invited me to join him on deck up front. I was sure my sandals didn't have the suction cup grips Bob's feet did, so, as gracefully as possible, I butt-shuffled from the back of the boat to the front of the boat. Once there my friend and I sat on the bow surveying the spectacular palate of autumn's colors splashed among the green hills that held the river and us. It was wonderful.

In time, I began to relax and, yes, even enjoy the experience of sailing. In fact Kim and I slept in the modest cabin of the boat that night. The gentle rocking coupled with the soft lapping sounds of the river kissing the hull put me in a sound sleep. No nightmares.

Unlike most other forms of transportation, sailing is not about getting somewhere fast, unless you happen to be involved in a yacht race. Generally, sailing is not about taking the most direct route anywhere. It's about giving one's self over to the wind to experience a meandering journey.

Learning to Meander

As I embark on the second half of my life's journey and reflect on these first forty-plus years, I confess that I have spent way too much time trying to get somewhere else in a hurry. Driving, high school graduation, college, another graduation, marriage, graduate school, another graduation, being appointed to one church and then the next and the next and the next, as I traveled along what I thought was the path to success. I wanted to get to the next event in my life as quickly as possible. I wanted to be perceived by others as someone important. I was eager to do something spectacular for the kingdom of God. So I stormed the gates of every opportunity that presented itself, dragging those I loved, and supposedly served, behind me white knuckled and red faced. And each time I impulsively jumped at the chance to do anything that would further my ambitions, I failed to do the difficult work of discerning whether it was the place God wanted me to be and whether I had the gifts, graces, or calling to be there.

Just a few short years ago I became willing to face this side of myself. As is so often the case, personal hardship helped to peel away the scales from my eyes. The death of my mother, the loss of some of my closest friends and staff, a financial crisis that threatened the very survival of our young church, and the discovery of some of the darker sides of myself bubbling up to the surface of my stress-laden life threatened to be the death of me. Fortunately, not everything was hopeless. My wife and sons were a stabilizing presence for me, like the keel of the sailboat that enables it to sail virtually on its side without capsizing. Still, I know how wet they got standing so close to my kicking and flailing.

This book is about my own journey from life to death and back to life again. It's the story of a person, probably much like you, who wonders, "Why couldn't I have accepted myself—my strengths, gifts, *and* limitations—earlier on in this first stage of my life? Why couldn't I have trusted more in God's Spirit to guide me?" Maybe it is true that the most valuable of life's lessons rarely arrive according to our schedules and most often become apparent to us when we are way too wet or worn out to deny them. In any event, I am glad to have arrived at this new sense of self-awareness and with it this desire to live life in a much more spiritually discerning and meandering way.

This book is also an invitation to journey into the depths of your own soul and to consider following the Spirit's lead in the next chapters of your life.

When was the last time you journeyed somewhere? I don't mean a trip where you raced to get from point A to point B in the least amount of time. I mean a journey where the destination itself was not nearly as important as the experience of getting there? We don't do journeys very well, do we? We are in way too much of a hurry.

Living in central Florida in "the land of the worlds" (Disney World, SeaWorld, and the like) I see continual proof of this. It's funny how people will travel halfway across the world, spend thousands of dollars on airline tickets and hotel accommodations, only to drag themselves and their families at breakneck speed from one park to the next to the point of vacation overload. All of this because they need a break from their own daily experience of a finger-gripping, red-faced rat race.

As Florida residents we have annual passes that allow us into all the popular parks. We have already learned the best times of the week to visit these parks and, more important, when to stay far, far away. My wife and I can spot a driven tourist family a mile away. Weary parents with a death grip on their children's arms quickly walking to the next family fun-filled attraction in cadence with their constant barrage of accusations and threats. "You are so spoiled. I am never taking you on vacation again. Wait until I get you back in the room." Ah, the joyful sounds of families on the vacation of their lives. I have been there. Chances are you have too.

We are so driven as individuals that even our dream vacations fall victim to the tyranny of the urgent. With straight-line determination, we plan to get what we want and where we want without any thought that the detours and setbacks we will encounter along the way may very well be the better part of the journey. When learning to sail, I had to understand and execute a maneuver called "tacking." Sailboats cannot sail directly into the wind in straight-line fashion, so you have to tack, or zigzag, into the wind to get where you want to go. Unless a sailor is willing to do this, the boat may flounder or be driven terribly off course. In the same way, when we are driven to force our way forward, we may end up frustrated and off course from where the Spirit seeks to lead us, which is often the long and more winding way.

We tend to overdirect and oversteer our lives, all the while keeping our sails neatly furled and tucked away for fear that the wind may take us to places we did not plan to go. How often we settle for sitting white knuckled and red faced doing it all our own way rather than taking the risk of unfurling the sails of our deepest selves to catch the gusts of the Spirit. But it's precisely in the wind of the Spirit that we find our soul's breath and are more naturally led, rather than driven, to the greatest destinations life has in store for us.

I have become more open to following the Spirit's leading in my life. Working to make my own personal shift from success-oriented drivenness to a more significance-oriented meandering style of life, I am beginning to discover a deeper sense of joy and satisfaction in my life and ministry.

Learning to loosen my grip on life and a ministry calling that compels me and to simply slow down the pace of my journey is helping me to see with new eyes and hear with new ears the quiet and unobtrusive presence of God around me. My sails are beginning to billow. I am finding myself being led to places around me—but, more important, within me—that I never knew were there, or perhaps I have simply forgotten them in the midst of my white-knuckled busyness.

You won't find in these pages a neatly outlined formula for deepening intimacy with God. And you won't discover a carefully laid out plan for revitalizing your vocation or ministry. This is not another "how to" book. You probably have enough of those sitting on your shelf unread. What you will find here are reflections from a fellow traveler and some valuable lessons learned from trying to race through life and ministry from one success to another and discovering, by more intentionally opening the sails of my heart through the harsh desert experience of pain, a more grace-filled, Spirit-led way.

This book is your own personal invitation to learn how to sail—to join the journey from success-oriented drivenness to significance-oriented meandering. That is, to take the winding way through life and slow down enough to learn some things about yourself and God along the way. Perhaps even to learn how to sail in your own desert. Welcome aboard! And leave the suction cup shoes behind.

1

The Meandering Way

My wife and I recently celebrated our 25th wedding anniversary by indulging in a much-anticipated cruise. We had tried and failed numerous times since our 10th anniversary to take this cruise. Finally, however, after moving this trip to the top of our things-to-do list and successfully meeting our financial goals, we were off to the Caribbean on our five-day adventure. We decided this vacation would be an opportunity to do things we wouldn't ordinarily do. On our first attempt to be daring, we signed up for an excursion that included speedboats and snorkeling. An unusual combination for us to be sure.

With my wife sitting behind me, holding on for dear life in our two-seat speedboat, we quickly accelerated across the water. The typically glasslike surface around the Cayman Islands had yielded to choppier waters this day, with three- and four-foot swells. Our guide took great pleasure goading his unsuspecting tourists far away from shore. I know he was probably only going about 15 miles per hour as we followed him in our 25 horsepower motor boats, but the waves made it feel a lot faster. We hit our first swell full throttle and were launched into the air, landing hard on the next swell. From behind me, I heard a loud, "Woo-hoo!" My wife was loving it. Seeing that his landlubber clan was keeping up with him, our guide decided to notch things up a bit and started zigzagging across the waves. Not wanting my manhood to be questioned, I hit the throttle and followed. As we continued skipping across the waves, bouncing left and right, I could feel my heart pounding in my throat. I was pretty much scared to death. My earliest fears of the water were welling up within me, but I struggled successfully to push them aside. I kept telling myself, rather unconvincingly, "This is fun!"

After 20 minutes, when everyone caught up with our guide, we grouped our boats together and killed the motors. Our guide gave us a quick lesson on snorkeling. This was our first time at this, so we listened intently, all the while bobbing up and down on the waves. My wife tried her best to push the feeling away, but an impeding wave of seasickness was coming on her. As soon as the lesson was over, green faced and fully geared, she slipped over the side of our boat and into the water. She managed to keep it together for about 20 minutes before making her way back to the boat to empty the contents of her stomach into the sea. Being the sympathetic person that I am (not!), I wished I had a camera to catch the moment. My better nature, however, led me to ask one of the guides to take us back to shore, cutting our adventure short. We spent the rest of our expensive two-hour excursion sitting at a picnic table where our tour began, recovering our wits and eventually laughing about the whole event. So much for our fast-paced adventure. With the few hours we had remaining on the island we enjoyed wandering in and out of the shops in town. We agreed we were designed for a much slower pace.

That evening, as I reflected on the pace of my life in general, I made this entry in my journal: "When did I become in such a hurry? Why do I so easily throttle up to a near hectic speed most days of my life? When did drivenness supplant my sense of purpose in life? Why do I feel like I have to do so much? When will enough be enough? How long am I going to be able to sustain this pace?"

Learning to Drive

In a world of fast food, quick service, and express lanes, we tend to hurry more and accomplish less. We manage to get from point A to point B much faster now than we did 10 years ago. And if we happen to slow down or, heaven forbid, stop for even a moment, we quickly become uncomfortable and start looking around for the next task, project, or place we ought to be. This hectic pace of life exacts its price on us. By attempting to cram more and more activity into our already busy lives we inadvertently neglect our own need for rest, reflection, and renewal.

A pastor friend of mine was recently granted a generous renewal leave from the church he serves. He has been working at this church for more than a dozen years and has been complaining lately about being on the brink of burnout. He has confided in me numerous times that his family has suffered from his workaholic tendencies. He mourns the loss of relationships he could have had with his children had he worked less at the church. He lamented how his relationship with his wife has become only civil at best. Though my friend admitted all of this to himself, and to me, the pace of his life remains virtually unchanged. He regularly downs megadoses of vitamins to boost his immune system so he can keep going. After receiving this gift of renewal, he began stressing out about all the time he will have with "nothing" to do. He has neglected his need for rest, reflection, and renewal for so long that he is now threatened by them. I wouldn't be surprised if he finds an excuse for delaying this opportunity.

As someone who is also by nature a type-A driven personality, I have come to despise the fact that I too tend to move along at such an unhealthy pace. Even as I write this chapter on a laptop computer the size of a small book with a processor faster than the computers carried on board the earliest space flights, I realize the price I am paying for speed, convenience, and portability—mainly more time for more work and less time for other things. I know I ought to recoup the time I save for other things like prayer, introspection, and more restful activities but I don't. It's my own fault. What was supposed to lighten my workload and give me more leisure time has only helped me to labor at a faster pace.

I also have this love-hate relationship going with my pocket personal data assistant (PDA) as well. On the one hand, it feels good to be organized. Meetings logged in their tiny spaces. My electronic things-to-do list, neatly prioritizing all the things I need to accomplish. I even have two different versions of the Bible inside this tiny case, so instead of relying on my memory or thumbing through the thin white pages, I type in a word, hit a button, and dozens of references pop up, suggesting the verses I am looking for. All of this makes me more efficient, for sure. I guess I am free to use my brain cells for other things besides remembering important meeting dates and Bible references. And because I have all these modern technological devices at my disposal, I have little excuse for being disorganized or for-getting about a meeting. I have the tools to be more efficient. My life neatly and carefully unfolds, one planned activity at a time, 10 hours a day. And I am left to wonder, "Is this really a *good* thing?"

I am becoming much more aware of the pace at which I live my life. Lately, I have been observing myself at the office, especially when I am interrupted by others. I notice that usu-ally when someone catches me off guard in the hallway, as I am rushing from one meeting or activity to the next, I don't really tune in to what the person is saying. I am standing there acting like I am listening while my mind is somewhere else. And I have noticed my feet too. Usually I have one foot pointing toward whatever direction I intend to head next, ready to bolt at the first opportunity I find.

At what point along the way did I begin to embrace driven-ness as a virtue? And when did I begin to justify this fast-paced lifestyle as a quality pleasing to God, then hold it up as a model for others to follow?

While I am sure I had tendencies toward drivenness as a child, they didn't fully emerge until around age 18 when I became the pastor of a small inner-city church. I knew nothing about pastoral ministry. Prior to this I had never preached a sermon, taught a Sunday school class, or led or even attended an administrative meeting. I had only attended one funeral (and that was for my grandfather), had never been in a hospital, and had no clue what it meant to lead people spiritually. You could say I was somewhat of an oddity back then—this passionate young man with a strong calling to serve God, willing to work in a city church without a clue about what it means to be a pastor.

People admired someone my age with the courage to be doing this ministry. I got a lot of positive affirmation for my hard work and commitment. My superiors repeatedly told me I was a rising star and that if I continued on the track I was on, I would eventually serve a large church or become a leader in our denomination. It was all so very seductive to someone who had been afflicted up until then with an inferiority complex. The positive strokes I was getting made me want to live up to everything everyone else saw in me. I didn't want to let anyone down, so I became driven to make others' vision for me a reality.

Throughout my formative years in ministry I seemed to seek out situations that reinforced this drivenness to succeed, to be what others wanted me to be. I volunteered to be on numerous denominational committees and task forces so that I could see the inner workings of the church and be seen as someone effective and worthy of his calling. I easily overextended myself by trying to please others and live up to their image, one I had embraced for myself.

Just out of seminary, I was appointed by our bishop to serve what is called a three-point circuit. That simply means I was the pastor of three different congregations at one time. These churches were nestled in the hills of three Appalachian communities in north-central Pennsylvania. My immediate superior defined this circuit as "the worst appointment in the worst district of our annual conference." What a great introduction to one's new ministry!

I was so driven to do something spectacular there that I jumped at the chance to get involved in as many church and community ministries and programs as possible. By the end of my sixth year of ministry, I had directed a youth center, clothing bank, and food bank; served as a volunteer ambulance attendant; cofounded a hospice; started one of our nation's first Students Against Drunk Driving chapters; worked with the local school board; served as our district youth coordinator overseeing regionwide events for more than three hundred students; chaired several judicatory committees; and served three congregations. As if this wasn't enough, in my fourth year of ministry I entered a doctoral program at a university four hours away and commuted two days a week to classes. In this drivenness I accomplished a great deal and received lots of recognition for service rendered.

Unfortunately, much of what I read and experienced in the wider church market only fueled this sense of drivenness in me. How many times I have heard in popular church-growth seminars that the most successful pastors are the ones who are driven. They eat, sleep, dream, and live for the church. The leaders of these events may not have said that in so many words, but when I listened to the stories they told about their own ministries, the message came through loud and clear. According to some of them, to be effective in ministry I have to be a visionary leader, personally visit every first-time guest of the church within 24 hours, pray several hours a day, read a book a week, journal, study scripture daily, belong to an accountability group, direct the staff, take my wife on a date once a week, connect with other pastors in the local ministerial association, belong to a group like the Rotary, and complete and return all the forms my conference requires of me on a weekly basis. I confess that I attempted to do much of this.

Years later I was the founding pastor of a new congregation in western Pennsylvania. Because 70 percent of all new churches planted in the United States fail in the first three years, I was driven to succeed in being one of the 30 percent that not only survived but thrived. I was willing to do almost anything to grow the church. Because I found tremendous purpose in being a church-planting pastor, I easily justified any sense of drivenness on my part as simply one of the necessities of this particular calling in life.

I have been in seven different pastoral ministry settings since I graduated from high school. I have to confess that in most of these I have been driven by other than what one might consider holy desires—to be the best preacher and counselor, have the best church, be the best consultant, be a success. But by whose standards? In spite of the ways I found encouragement for my driving habits, much of my own personal experience has been that any success born of drivenness usually comes at a pretty hefty cost to one's marriage, family, personal health, and faith.

Not until my sixth ministry setting, having planted Cornerstone Church in western Pennsylvania, was I forced to confront many of these demons. Prior to this I bought into the promise that by working 70 hours a week, following a few scripted rules, a clear formula for success, and a carefully written five-year plan of action, I would soon be sitting pretty in a church of one thousand or more people with a large, effective staff to lead them. Driven to succeed, I intended to lead the church from point A to point B to point C, and so on, to become everything I desired it to be. I was driven to do all the "right" things, use all the "right" strategies, follow all the "right" rules. Five years into my journey at Cornerstone, we were not even close to where I thought we would be.

Looking back, I would have to say that isn't necessarily a bad thing. My failure to achieve all that I had set out to accomplish at Cornerstone helped me to see that church growth and vitality aren't something I could make happen no matter how driven I would be. And that such driving was hindering my own spiritual growth. In this period of intense struggle, I wrote in my journal, "Is it possible that this opportunity to plant a new congregation really has little to do with growing a church and more to do with growing me?" I was beginning to see that left unchecked, my drivenness, no matter how purposeful, could diminish or defeat the greater intentions God had to grow me into the kind of person God intends me to be.

In Paul's letter to the Galatians he presents this promise and challenge: "By contrast, the fruit of the Spirit is love, joy, peace, patience, kindness, generosity, faithfulness, gentleness, and self control" (Gal. 5:22). In my attempts to do ministry "right," I drove myself very hard, and in spite of this drivenness the evidence of God's fruit in me was lacking. I have learned since then that just as we cannot force fruit to grow on trees or on the vine, we cannot force the fruit of the Spirit to grow in us. Much the same way fruit trees grow naturally when they are exposed to the sun and avail themselves of the nutrients of the earth, the fruits of the Spirit develop naturally in our lives when we regularly avail ourselves to God.

Aspiring now to avail myself more to the Spirit, I am actively working to recover from my own drivenness. I am truly becoming less desirous now of doing something spectacular *for* God and much more committed to doing something significant *with* God. This shift has opened me more fully to being faithful to what and who I am called to be in this moment. I am slowly finding that I desire the fruit of the Spirit to be the measure of my relationships with people rather than how effectively I can drive them toward the accomplishment of whatever goal I have for the church.

So What's Driving You?

Much has been written in the past few years about the virtues of being driven. Many churches have latched onto widely popular "driven" resources and their various spin-off products in an attempt to reinvigorate themselves. Pastor Rick Warren of Saddleback Church in California has sold millions of copies of his books *The Purpose-Driven Church* and *The Purpose-Driven Life* with the intent to reacquaint individual Christians, and the universal church, with the primary purposes for which they were created. Warren believes that worship, fellowship, discipleship, mission, and faith-sharing are the primary purposes for which God created us. While I don't personally subscribe to the deterministic theology behind much of Warren's work, which basically asserts that God causes everything good and bad that happens in our lives, I do appreciate his attempts to help individuals and the corporate church affirm or rediscover their sense of purpose.

Like Warren, I too believe each of us has many wonderful purposes in life. I find great purpose in being a husband, father, pastor, and friend. Part of the joy of life is to find purpose in all the arenas of our lives and to help others do the same. Who we are and what we do purposefully, especially in our relationships, makes a difference in our lives and the world around us. For example, if I am purposeful about living out the Spirit-fruit of kindness, then I will work to become an advocate for kindness in my marriage, my workplace, my faith community, and the wider world.

I had the opportunity to serve bottled water at a local rally for immigration rights. I knew the issue was a divisive one and that well-meaning and faith-filled people would stand on both sides of the many issues surrounding the presence of illegal immigrants in our country. Because I find a purpose in performing random acts of kindness, I joined nearly a dozen other people from our church to simply act kindly toward those who would be at this rally. I knew it might not make me popular with some folks, but then I didn't do this to be popular. When people asked me which side of the issue I was supporting, I simply replied, "The thirsty!" I had a purpose that day. It was simply to offer kindness in the form of bottled water to anyone who happened to need a drink.

From the time I was a young child, I have valued being kind toward others. At age six, I used to walk up and down Pine Street, where I lived in Milton, Delaware, and visit the widows who lived nearby. My parents thought I went there for the cookies and milk they gave me, but it was deeper than that for me. I felt sorry that these women lived alone. I visited them simply because I thought they needed a little kindness. The goodies they gave me, however, were a wonderful side benefit to my compassion.

When I was 10 years old our family moved to a large town in New Jersey just across the river from Philadelphia and a rough place wrought with racial tension and violence. It was here that I first came upon a homeless person. Having grown up in a small tight-knit community where I sensed everyone had a home and was cared for by people who loved them, I found it difficult to grasp the idea of someone being homeless. So whenever I happened upon someone like that, I brought them to my home. I would regularly surprise my mother by walking into our kitchen with a complete stranger in tow. My mother, who understood and appreciated my tender heart, would welcome our guest and quickly cook up something for them to eat. Though my mother cautioned me regularly about the dangers of approaching these strangers, she did so in a way that did not squelch my kindness.

Seeing joy in the faces of the widow women on Pine Street and watching hungry strangers enjoy a hot meal at my kitchen table somehow gave me a sense of purpose. I felt, even as a kid, that I could make a difference in someone else's life.

Opening ourselves to experiences that grant us a sense of purpose is a healthy and holy thing. However, when we allow ourselves to become driven in them, we may find our sense of purpose diminished—what was once an activity or action that flowed out of purposefulness and love has now become a compulsion, something we have to do, one more thing to accomplish. Like acid eats away at something you expose to it, drivenness often eats away at our sense of purpose.

Mark Buchanan, a pastor and freelance writer out of Canada who himself has wrestled with the tension between purpose and drivenness in his own life, says in his book *The Rest of God:* "A common characteristic of driven people is that at some point they forget their purpose. They lose the point. The very reason they began something—embarked on a journey, undertook a project...entered a profession, married a woman—erodes under the weight of striving."[1] In other words, if we are not careful, our drivenness may unseat the very purpose we have in life.

There was a time when my drivenness would have had me out in front at that immigration rally, promoting myself and my church. I would have worn a shirt with our church name blazoned across my chest. I would have had water bottles with our church logo and Web site on the label. For fear of having to share the limelight with others, I wouldn't have partnered with other social service agencies or non-Christian organizations. I would have been driven to use the event to gain name recognition for my particular congregation. In the drivenness of it all, I would have lost sight of my purpose for being there—giving water to the thirsty. By God's persistent grace, I was just one person among many, simply passing out water. That simple act of kindness, for the sake of those who were thirsty and not for myself, reminded me of the purpose I felt as a child visiting the widow women of Pine Street.

Unfortunately, "driven" all too often defines our modern life. We are driven in almost everything we do. Don't believe me? Take a look at some of the activities you find yourself regularly involved in. How often are you—at heart—driven to accomplish? Driven to perfection? Driven to succeed? Driven to advance? Driven to please others? Driven to control situations? Driven to do something good for others? Driven to experience and keep the peace in your family? Driven to help others move along in their spiritual journey? Driven to accomplish everything on your things-to-do list? Driven to be your child's best friend? Driven to be liked by everyone you know? Driven to be something other than who you are right now? Think about the last time you bought gas for your car, stood in line at the grocery store, got your family ready for a worship service, went on vacation, visited someone in the hospital, wrote a sermon, or ran into a friend you hadn't seen for a while. Did you enjoy the moment, or were you driven to get on to the next thing on your list of things to do, to find a way to grab center stage, to hide yourself from someone you knew just to avoid conversation, to make a good impression and miss the opportunity to experience a greater purpose in the moment?

My father-in-law loved this saying: "Great peace lies at the center of personal insignificance." There was a time in my striving to succeed, to "be" someone, when that saying made no sense at all. As I am learning to embrace my purposes in life and to slow the pace down, I am feeling much more at peace knowing that the whole world doesn't rest on my shoulders or revolve around me. That the problems I face as a pastor were there before me and, most likely, will be there when I am gone. I am fairly certain that my in-basket will not be emptied before I die. So why go on living as though it all depends on me? Why drive myself so hard to get it all done today?

More than once on our cruise my wife and I commiserated about just how quickly time has passed since we first met. Important things, purposeful things, like going to school, serving multiple churches, raising children, and sometimes working extra jobs to make ends meet seemed to have accelerated the pace, and the stress, of our lives. After 26 years of marriage and a renewed commitment to each other, we are more than ready now to find a different way to navigate the remainder of our journeys here on earth. Life is far too stressful to be compounding it with the anxiety, pressure, and pain of drivenness. I am slowly finding a better way, a healthier way to live life as God intends, in what I now call a more meandering way.

Discovering the Meandering Way

"To meander" simply means to take a winding course. Meandering is like taking a casual stroll on the beach—stopping to look for shells, watching the sandpipers play "dodge the waves," smelling the misty fragrance of the salt air, and soaking up the rays of the sun. Meandering is like walking leisurely through a forest around rocks and tree stumps following the contours of a crooked, mossy path. I am deeply indebted to a few special people in my life who modeled this meandering pace for me long before I was ready to embrace it.

Ed and Barb Shultz are two of these special people for me. Cancer claimed them at a much-too-early age, but their spirits and the meandering lessons they left behind are etched indelibly in my heart. When I first met them, I thought them odd. Who in their right minds spends a Saturday morning well before sunrise sitting on a damp rock ledge looking through binoculars for bald eagles? What kind of person spends a Sunday afternoon walking at a snail's pace through the woods—one looking up to catch a glimpse of whatever bird was warbling away in the trees while the other was looking down to find a trillium, jack-in-the-pulpit, or fern? I regret that I used to merely tolerate these outings just to be near their daughter. But in spite of myself, something of their meandering spirit infected me.

Now there is nothing I enjoy more than being outdoors. I find myself drawn to nature, trying to see what my in-laws were looking for and found for themselves. They discovered that when we avail ourselves to the vastness of creation, we have a much better perspective on life. That problem we allow to ruin our sleep or the worrisome thought we let rob us of our best daydreams; the desire to do something spectacular, to overextend ourselves at work, or to become something greater than we already are begins to shrink under the immenseness of everything that surrounds us.

How we experience this meandering way is unique to our own personality styles and preferences. For example, as an extroverted and fairly laid-back guy, I experience and enjoy meandering in a way very different from my wife, Kim, who is introverted and very structured. I like to hang out at the beach, fish, sail, and be with lots of people. Kim enjoys reading, spending time alone, and organizing things. When we vacation together we have to negotiate our activities so that both of our needs are met.

What is important about meandering is the pace and focus individuals bring to whatever activity or task we are involved in. Whether we are working at our desks, doing something outdoors, reading a good book, listening to great music, or reflecting on a painting or sculpture, meandering allows us to be more engaged in the task and to soak up more of the experience of the moment. Unlike drivenness—getting somewhere fast or accomplishing our goals the quickest way possible— meandering slows us down and helps us appreciate the here and now, where we are in the journey, what we are experiencing, and who might be walking beside us.

I don't want you to misunderstand what I am saying here. Meandering is not an excuse for laziness or irresponsibility. I know I am responsible for accomplishing many things each day. People are counting on me to do my best in a timely manner. I also know that these things are important and deserving of my best efforts. Meandering generally requires that I slow down, but it has less to do with the speed or efficiency with which I accomplish the goals and tasks I set for myself and more to do with the attitude or posture with which I approach these things. Meandering is ultimately about openness to the gifts God seeks to bestow on us for our own well-being. For example, my pastor friend who was offered an eight-week leave from his church for personal renewal and reflection is such a workaholic that he runs the risk of approaching this time with such reluctance and resentment that it may actually do him more harm than good. He may physically slow down, stay out of the office, and away from the phone, but unless he adjusts his attitude and posture toward his renewal leave he will most likely fill his days and weeks with other kinds of stressful busyness and drivenness. Clergy are vulnerable to the self-abuses of drivenness, but they are not alone. Here in central Florida I see many families who come for the vacation of a lifetime only to stress themselves out by rushing around to do it all, get their money's worth, and, if it kills them, have a great time.

When we are running full tilt, finding or maintaining a meandering posture is difficult. When we are absorbed in problems or driven to accomplish so many things—even worthwhile things—being open to the gifts God has for us in each day is hard. For example, when I feel driven to do something, I usually approach the task with a kind of fixed sight and closed-handedness. With determination, I seal myself off from everything around me and move forward like a soldier advancing to take a hill. I am not looking for distractions. In fact, I am determined to shut them out. I am not interested in guidance. I know what I want to do, and I am set to do it.

When I meander, I approach things with a spirit of openness. "Great peace lies at the center of personal insignificance." I look around to survey the landscape. I may explore pathways that diverge from the road I am on. I look for others who are on the journey and ask them about their experiences along the way. I am open to others' guidance. I know where I want to go but understand there may be many different ways to get there. I look at my time off from work as an opportunity for renewal, not as an extension of my workweek when I can catch up on all the things I wanted to get done. Vacations become graced periods to detach myself fully from the busyness of my life. Moments of rest and reflection throughout the day become invitations to lift my eyes beyond the computer screen or the desk in front of me, to cast my vision far enough ahead to see the birds riding effortlessly on the wind.

When our sons were in elementary school, my wife and I decided to take them on a two-week adventure through Colorado and Wyoming. We funded our trip with the small inheritance my wife received from her parents' estate. For the first time we were able to go on vacation without counting every penny we spent. Instead of using a travel agent to plan this trip, I decided to use the Internet. I calculated the distances I thought we could travel each day without tiring ourselves. I pulled up pictures of potential places to stay, compared amenities, and booked our accommodations. With the exception of our first night at a buffalo ranch near Cheyenne, Wyoming, our plans went off without a hitch. Because we knew where we were heading each day, had plenty of time to get there, and had mapped out all the appropriate routes, we discovered we could take little side trips that often led us to some of the most spectacular sights we had ever seen.

I will never forget the day we were heading north on Route 25 from Cheyenne to Casper when we saw a well-worn sign for Ayers Natural Bridge Park. We quickly made the turn that led us along several miles of dirt road to one of the most beautiful places on earth. We spent an hour wading in the cool, natural spring in our bare feet. And we sat on the lush, green grass finding faces in the clouds. We reluctantly got back in the car and headed back toward Casper. I am so glad we meandered that day to a place that still remains fresh in our hearts.

Each week I know where I am headed in my work and have all my tasks neatly mapped out for me. I know that I have five days to take care of all the things I need to accomplish. Yet what I cannot foresee are all the detours—the little interruptions I will face from coworkers who want to run ideas by me or members who will come looking for guidance in moments of crisis. To keep myself from lapsing back into a closed-handed kind of drivenness, I try to remain open to the side trips that present themselves along the way. I have even incorporated some of these side trips into my schedule—a kind of planned spontaneity.

For example, there was a time in ministry when sermon preparation was a real burden for me. In my drivenness to do it right, whatever "right" means, I would go to various workshops and seminars on preaching and return home with my head full of everyone else's ideas about how it should be done. I would try to emulate some of the "successful" speakers I had heard. But, in my drivenness to do it right, I had lost my voice—the unique and wonderful story I was called to share with the congregation I serve. Someone in the church finally took me aside one Sunday morning and gently encouraged me to be myself. For me that meant discovering my own process for sermon development and finding my own voice for sharing the good news.

As a result, sermon preparation has slowly become a meandering experience for me. Here's what I typically do now. Each quarter I will meet with the other two pastors from our church to begin sermon planning. In addition to scheduling who will be preaching and when, we discuss topical sermon series and passages of Scripture to go along with them. First thing Monday morning each week, I prayerfully think about the predetermined theme for the coming Sunday's sermon. I develop a general idea of what I want to convey in my message and scribble out some thoughts on a notepad. I look for resources in my office that will help me develop my theme—commentaries, illustrations, excerpts from books I have been reading. I try to identify personal experiences I have had that help to convey the message I want to share. I begin to organize my thoughts. Then Wednesday and Thursday mornings I pack up all my stuff, visit one of the local coffeehouses, and set up shop. (I am at one of these coffee shops right now as I write this chapter.) I will spend three or four hours each of these mornings working on my sermon and—here is where part of the meandering comes in for me—as I write I will look up and, scanning the room, ask questions in my head of the people who walk by: What would this mean to you? Would you get this illustration? How relevant is this to your life in this fast-paced suburb of Orlando?

Rather than driving to get the sermon written as quickly as possible, I purposely slow the pace down, get out of the office and into the community I am seeking to serve, and routinely invite others into the process. Meandering for me in this context has less to do with the amount of time I spend writing my sermons each week and more to do with the attitude and posture in which I approach this work.

In my previous church setting, I visited the same Starbucks in town for three years and got to know many of the team members by name. They eventually caught on to what I was doing there each week and would sometimes stop and ask me, "Whatcha working on this week, Pastor?" And I would pitch my message to them and ask for their feedback. Those particular sermons were always the best.

I am learning, slowly, that a meandering attitude and posture in life is so much healthier for me than drivenness. I am much more relaxed in the work I do. I enjoy time off and time away from my job. I find the time I spend with others so much more delightful. And I am experiencing a greater openness to the Spirit, who seeks continually to fill my life with God's presence and love. In all these ways, and more, meandering has lightened my life and enlivened my spirit.

So I guess there's a lot to be said for people who sit on rocks in the predawn hours looking for bald eagles. And there is definitely something to be said for coming to terms with our own insignificance and trusting instead the power and grace of God to sustain the world and you and me. This is nothing new. Two thousand years ago someone came to show us this meandering way.

Jesus, a Model Meanderer

I think Jesus showed the way of meandering better than anyone else. Jesus knew where he was going and why. The Gospel writer Luke noted how, near the end of his earthly life, Jesus "set his face to go to Jerusalem" (Luke 9:51). A cross was waiting for him, and he determined to meet it. No one and nothing could keep Jesus from fulfilling the ultimate purpose of his life.

However, as we read the Gospel accounts of Jesus's life, we see that Jesus never seemed to be in much of a hurry. I don't get the sense that he was driven by anyone. Wherever he was, he was fully present. He met each person and circumstance with great attention. He lived his life with great intentionality.

Jesus taught, healed, conversed, traveled, and loved, but he was never in a hurry. He seemed to take his good old time getting to most places, often arriving late or not at all. His life and ministry had clear purpose and direction, and within that he opened himself to detours, side trips, and delays. And as he meandered, Jesus noticed simple things like flowers, sparrows, rocks, and fishermen. He tarried at weddings, cried at funerals, and filled his plate at banquets. Jesus recognized the Father's presence in some of the most mundane places, simply because he moved at a pace that actually allowed him to see. And out of his meandering came the most colorful of metaphors used for teaching. For example, "Look at the birds of the air; they neither sow nor reap nor gather into barns, and yet your heavenly Father feeds them. Are you not of more value than they?" (Matt. 6:26). And "Consider the lilies of the field, how they grow; they neither toil nor spin, yet I tell you, even Solomon in all his glory was not clothed like one of these. But if God so clothes the grass of the field, which is alive today and tomorrow is thrown into the oven, will he not much more clothe you?" (Matt. 6:28–30).

Now I know that seeing God has little to do with one's physical speed and everything to do with one's spiritual attentiveness. But you have to admit it is very difficult to be attentive to the things of God when you are moving through life at a breakneck pace. I think it is precisely because Jesus meandered and experienced life in slower motion that he was able to gather the rest, resources, and insights needed for the crafting of his thoughts and teachings.

Consider that only a fraction of the things Jesus said or did ever got recorded in the Gospels. If the Gospel writers record maybe a year's worth of Jesus's ministry, as some scholars suggest, that means a full two years' worth of his activity are not included. Why? Maybe it's because he spent so much time doing ordinary and seemingly insignificant things. Maybe a lot of his conversations just seemed plain unimportant to the Gospel writers. Perhaps they saw his casual encounters with simple folks as less significant than his miracles. Can't you see the nearly empty page in a disciple's journal at the end of the day? "Nothing worth noting today. Talked to a few people. Caught a couple fish. Skipped some stones on the lake. Horsed around with some children. Maybe tomorrow!" I know sometimes my journal entries are a lot like that.

I believe it was precisely because of the time Jesus spent meandering with others, and the Father, that he so aptly understood the human heart and was able to so quickly build relationships of trust. Nothing in his meandering day was wasted. Everything he did had purpose.

The times I have felt most satisfied, refreshed, creative, and purposeful in life and ministry have been the times when, like Jesus, I have intentionally altered the pace of my life so that I could take more time to simply meander with God and others.

Each time I have done this, I have found myself more spiritually centered and ultimately more focused in my work.

From Heartache to Hope

Sometimes, without our prompting, life will alter the pace for us. The birth of a child, a promotion at work, sickness, marriage, divorce, the death of someone we love—these things make us stop in our tracks. All forward motion ceases for a time. We would be wise in these moments to rest for a while and simply survey the landscape, find the horizon again, get a sense of where we are, and seek God's presence. Several years ago one of these painful experiences shattered my straight-course, driven life. My mother had been battling cancer for nearly two years, and suddenly the days, weeks, and months of slow physical deterioration quickly accelerated. My father called to tell me she had been admitted to the hospital for double pneumonia. I knew my mother was close to death. I made the trip from my home to the hospital in record time and arrived to find my mother in the critical care unit. She was conscious when I got there and surprised to see me. When I asked how she was feeling she said, "I'm a little weak but okay." And, as if to minimize her pain, she continued, "It's the chemotherapy. I always get like this after a treatment." It was true that her treatments exacted a price on her, but never like this. I knew she understood how serious this really was but she wasn't going to say it aloud. My mother was determined, like the scrappy young Philadelphia girl she once was, to beat this thing. When my mother made up her mind to do something, nothing could stand in her way. She was one of the most determined people I have ever known, and she believed, down to the final hours of her life, that she was going to emerge from this disease victorious. She did, of course, but not the way she had planned.

Five days after I arrived at the hospital to see her, my mom died. My dad, brother, and I were there to hold her while she took her last breath. Eyes that had been closed and still for nearly two days suddenly moved, as if straining to see through her eyelids, as if looking at something at a distance. Then a look of acceptance. Peace. We held her hands and prayed for God to receive her and to surround us with grace and peace.

I remember the drive back to my parents' house that morning. My dad quietly observed, "Everything just keeps moving along in the world. I feel like everything should be standing still right now, but it just keeps moving along." What he was noticing was that in the grand scheme of things, the loss of this person who has been so near and dear to us seemed inconsequential. Mom's life and death, which made such an incalculable difference in our life, seemed so small and insignificant compared with the drivenness of the world around us.

As painful as it was, however, my mother's death became the catalyst for some intense work in my life. In my drivenness I had lapsed into a kind of automatic pilot. Day after day, week after week, month after month, I kept an unhealthy pace. I got up early, worked way too late, and, to the neglect of my own well-being and that of my family, kept this unhealthy pace going. I had allowed ministry to become my life. It was predictable and controllable, and it gave me a sense of meaning and importance. What's not to love? Well, how about the feelings of loneliness, isolation, or shallowness it brought me?

My wife used to describe ministry as my mistress. She felt she had to compete with it for my time, my attention, and my affection. I came home one night to find her standing in the hallway of our home with her bags packed. She wasn't sure where she was heading, just away from me. I had a meeting I "needed" to get too. At the time it seemed urgent. Now I can't even remember what it was! How urgent could it have possibly been? Making up some lie to protect my image, I excused myself from the meeting. I went home and selfishly confronted my wife. "How could you do this to me? Don't you know how important this meeting is to the church's success (how about *my* success)? Why can't you understand how much this means to me?" I wish I could rewind that conversation and say some things differently, like "How could *I* do this to *you?* Why can't *I* understand how much this means to *you?*" To say the least, my priorities were horribly out of whack. It is a credit to my wife and her unwavering faithfulness that we are still married.

My life, which I have already characterized up to this point as driven, seemed to be collapsing around me. Those who knew me best noticed what they would have described as depression. Even my physician, whom I saw only once or twice that year, said he noticed something different about me. He discussed several treatment options. I told him I would swing out of it, that once I got back into the routine of life, especially the rigors of work, I would be back to my old self again. But the hole I found myself in was getting deeper and darker.

Other people I know who have experienced depression describe it as feeling drawn into a hole you can't get out of, no matter how much you want to or try. People who don't understand depression say things like "Do something to make yourself feel better" or "Quit thinking about yourself and do something for someone else in need" or "Do something you really enjoy." When you are depressed, you might really want to do these things. You just can't. My mother's death was one of many deaths I would experience over the next several months.

I was just beginning to learn an important truth: as an act of grace and kindness, God allows us to experience intense periods of suffering and pain. And although our nature is to fight against this, we trust that with God's grace and love for us, the pain we endure will help us grow in breathtaking ways we cannot yet imagine.

Questions for Reflection

1. How would you characterize the pace of your life right now?
2. What are some signs of drivenness in your life? Of meandering?

3. How would you describe the various purposes of your life?

4. Think about all the experiences that have shaped your journey in the deepest and most lasting ways. How many of them did you anticipate? How many did you make happen by drivenness or determination? How many came as seeming inconveniences or disruptions to your life? What you have learned about God through these experiences?

2

The Spirit's Leading

After my mother died I stood still long enough to realize that—like a sailing ship without a rudder—I was being pulled by a strong current, a depression I could not steer my way out of. Sailing into what had become uncharted waters for me, I was losing sight of land. I needed someone to help me navigate this journey. I decided to seek help through counseling. Talking with my therapist once a week was like ducking behind an island to get out of the wind and find the stability I needed. Tuesdays at 2:00 p.m. became my favorite time of the week. I would meet with my counselor for 45 minutes and follow up my sessions with a visit to a coffee shop to indulge myself in a fattening drink. I would sip it as slowly as possible and savor the insights I had gained about myself or about some challenge the counseling offered me that day. I would write about these things in my journal as a way to affirm them for myself.

In this time dedicated to me, I learned new things about myself, about life, about God. I learned some new ways to live again: to find a healthier pace, to embrace the journey from heartache to hope. I have since relocated to central Florida and for the second time am in the process of planting a church. In my passion and sense of urgency about this work, I still sometimes get ahead of myself and God. I still get caught at times in my need to succeed, still try to rush things along rather than wait on the Spirit's leading.

I am trying to learn something at once both simple and incredibly difficult: the destination is not a place but a person—a person who loves me very much and more than anything wants to be with me along the journey of life. I am much more open these days to the idea that God isn't all that interested in getting me somewhere. God is just interested in getting me! This journey from drivenness to meandering requires an experienced guide, and God's Spirit is a most capable traveling companion.

One of my favorite journey stories from the Bible is the Israelites' expedition from Egypt to the promised land. Some of God's best work, I think. A trip that easily could have been made in less than 40 days, had they followed a straight line, took 40 years. They meandered. Their travel log must have resembled the kind of scribbled picture a two-year-old would draw. You have probably heard someone explain their meanderings in this way: "More important than getting the Israelites out of Egypt was getting Egypt out of the Israelites." Or "The Israelites were lost because Moses wouldn't stop and ask for directions." I think their time spent wandering through the wilderness had more to do with God needing to spend quality time with the people (and the people with God) so they could experience God's faithfulness over and over again.

God wanted them to trust him *today.* That's why God provided manna on a daily basis. Consider the definition of *manna*—"What is it?" They had to trust God to know that this nameless, unidentifiable, perishable whatchamacallit would be enough for now. They were to gather up only what they could consume that day. If they tried to keep some of it overnight, it spoiled. Tomorrow God would provide—again. They couldn't make it happen—no matter how much they might be driven by hunger. They just had to meander around, collecting manna as it randomly fell from the sky.

But these ancient wanderers were a hardheaded bunch. How else can you explain them witnessing with their own eyes the 10 plagues, the parting of the sea (twice), bread from heaven, water from rocks, quail blown in by the wind, and countless kingdoms obliterated by the awesome power of God—only to whine, beg, and plead to go back to Egypt, back to a life of slavery, back to what was a familiar, linear, predictable way of life?

Maybe God needed 40 years to nurture a new generation of followers who might just "get" him and be willing to follow. Maybe what God wanted most from them, and now us, is a willingness to put one foot in front of the other, step after step, alongside him, no matter the pace or how the path might twist and turn. Maybe God wanted them to grasp a greater purpose for their lives—to be people who would give witness to this unique and awesome God.

Aren't we eager to get through whatever task or challenge we face in life as quickly as possible, moving steadily from point A to point B to point C, ever closer toward whatever goal we have in mind? The Israelites' experience reminds us: the spiritual journey doesn't work that way. In the faith journey, we are not so much racing toward a physical finish line as meandering toward becoming all that God has in mind for us to be. Like the Israelites, our ability to discern and follow God's leading has far less to do with time in a chronological sense and much more to do with direction.

Getting Our Clocks and Compasses in Sync

One of the plights of modern life is that we are all too often driven by the clock. Not so long ago I used to carry around an elaborate leather-bound organizer, a personal data assistant that fit into the leather organizer, a slim-line pocket calendar to tote around in my sport coat, and a chronograph watch on my wrist complete with day/date, dual time zones, and an alarm. Somehow, I thought all of these gadgets would help me manage my time more efficiently. They really meant I had more things to misplace. I recently shelved the organizer and ditched the slim-line pocket calendar, although I have not been able to wean myself away from my watches or my PDA. Still, I try not to allow myself to be driven so much by time and tasks.

Steven R. Covey, professor of business management and organization behavior, writes in his best-selling book *First Things First* about how fixated our culture is on the clock. The clock represents our busyness—commitments at work, appointments, tasks, and schedules. The clock symbolizes how we spend our lives. The compass, on the other hand, represents the personal vision, core values, and principles that shape and guide our lives. Covey suggests that we ought to rely more on the compass than the clock, because the compass has more to do with the direction we intend to follow on our journey.

The clock of our lives and the busyness it represents must always be servant of the compass, the vision and values directing our steps. True spiritual maturity comes when the clock and compass of our lives are in sync, when how I spend my time truly reflects what I most deeply value in life.

The Old Testament book of Jeremiah finds the people of Israel exiled in Babylon and restless for home. Their growing impatience made them susceptible to the false hope and promises propagated by some prophets who foretold an early release from captivity. These false promises fixated them on the clock. Like little children sitting in the back of the car on a long trip, they kept asking over and over again, "Hey, God, are we there yet?" Caught up in the clock, they lost sight of the compass. So God sent Jeremiah with the message, "For surely I know the plans I have for you, says the LORD, plans for your welfare and not for harm, to give you a future with hope" (Jeremiah 29:11). No timetable. No drivenness.

God's plan for the people was simple. Maybe that's why they missed it. Look at the next verses: "Then when you call upon me and come and pray to me, I will hear you. When you search for me, you will find me; if you seek me with all your heart, I will let you find me" (vv. 12–14). In other words, "When praying, listening, and looking for me become the focus of your lives, you will find me," says the Lord. "*I* am your future and your hope!"

The spiritual journey rarely unfolds in a straight line. We go forward and backward, left and right. We make progress, and we fall behind. Sometimes we feel like we are simply standing still. The questions we need to ask ourselves are not, how far have we come? (How long have we been on the road?) How much farther is it? (Or, when will we get there?) Those are clock questions. Rather, we need to ask, am I pointing myself in what I sense through the Spirit to be the right direction? Am I continually orienting myself toward God? Those are compass questions.

Getting Lost

Because of a childhood experience, there is no worse feeling in the world for me than the feeling of being lost. This is how I remember what happened.

The bell rang, signaling the end of another long week of school. I loved Fridays then almost as much as I do now. The seemingly endless tasks of first grade quickly yielded to a weekend of fishing, neighborhood Wiffle ball games, and building forts in the woods with friends. This Friday would be different. Miss Smith, my teacher, told me to wait at my desk while all the other kids noisily cleared the room.

I had about a two-mile walk from the elementary school to our home on Pine Street. Depending on what I would find to explore as I meandered through the small town of Milton, Delaware, it would take anywhere from forty-five minutes to an hour and a half to get home. My parents were used to my erratic arrival times.

After the last kid left the room, Miss Smith asked me to follow her to the car. She said she needed me to come home with her so we could have some time to practice for an upcoming school play. That was the first time I had heard anything about a play. I was hesitant to get in the car with her, but back in 1963 you didn't question the motives of your elders, especially people in authority like teachers.

Miss Smith was a single woman in her early 40s. I remember her as tall and slender with prematurely salt and peppered hair neatly pulled back into a ponytail accenting a thin smooth face. Her dark and piercing eyes gave the sense that she could read your thoughts.

We drove for about 20 minutes before arriving at her Victorian style home. I was too nervous to notice the direction we were heading. She ushered me into the living room where I sat quietly on an itchy red velour couch across from a grand piano. A pendulum wall clock loudly ticked away the minutes.

An hour went by and then two. There was no play rehearsal. No conversation. Just waiting and wondering. The sun was beginning to set as the knot of anxiety in the pit of my stomach tightened. The feeling of being lost scared me the most. Panic began to set in. Someone I trusted had betrayed me. Each time I called out to Miss Smith I was told, in a sharp-toned voice, to stay on the couch and remain quiet. I wanted my mom but had no way to tell her where I was or who I was with. I feared she might never find me. It was now quarter past six.

I heard the police car approaching before I could see its flashing lights. Another car was close behind. Their tires crackled on the oyster shell driveway common in our seaside town. A door slammed and then another. With each approaching footstep muffled voices grew louder, giving way to a sharp rap at the door. A heavyset police officer was the first to rush in. My mother, weaving her way around him, nearly fell into the room. Her eyes quickly darted left and right until she spotted me on the couch. I was quickly on my feet and by her side. After seeing that I was okay, she asked me to wait for her outside on the porch.

I could hear my mother and Miss Smith yelling at each other along with the deeper voice of the officer encouraging them to remain calm. My mother was the first to emerge from the house. She took my hand and pulled me aside as the officer escorted Miss Smith to his car. Miss Smith continued yelling at my mother, "You stole him from me. He's my son. You can't take him away from me!" My mother didn't offer me too many details about that incident except to say that Miss Smith was very ill and would have to be in the hospital for a long time. I later learned that Miss Smith, against her will, was admitted to a psychiatric hospital and removed from teaching. I never saw or heard from her again.

Scary experiences like that tend to burn themselves into our psyche like grooves on a record. To this day I still feel anxious when I sense I am lost and unable to find my way back home again. My heart beats faster and my palms become sweaty as a panicky feeling overtakes me.

Modern technology offers us a variety of resources to keep us from getting lost. Before moving to Orlando we needed to replace our minivan. We had come to the end of our seven-year plan to drive the wheels off it. The time had come to send it off to where thoroughly used cars go to die. After carefully considering our options we decided to buy another used van that had lots of features we normally wouldn't purchase like leather seats, power sliding doors, and a navigation system. Now that I have driven the car a while, I could live without the leather seats. They are brutal in the hot Florida sun. I could even do without the power doors. But the navigation system? It is true gift of God. We simply program in the address of our destination and a helpful female voice guides us carefully along our way. If we make a wrong turn she patiently tells us how to get back on track. We have our home address programmed into the computer so that anytime we get lost our friendly guide will lead us home.

No matter how careful we are there are still times when we encounter detours and dead ends and we suddenly find ourselves in unknown places. People we trust let us down. Promises made are not kept. Our drivenness takes us to places we would rather not be. Expectations we have of ourselves, God, and others are not met. We thought life would unfold one way only to find ourselves heading in the opposite direction. Difficulty and pain throw us off course until we are not sure how to find our way home. Sometimes we may even lose sight of *what* home is anymore.

While writing this chapter my closest friend died suddenly. An aneurysm took his life in a second. No chance for goodbyes.

We went back a long way. I was just out of seminary when Paul was assigned as my mentor. He was one of the people God used to shape and guide my life. He was only a few years older than I. Our families vacationed together. He baptized my oldest son. And though we lived 1,200 miles apart, we managed to stay in touch by phone and e-mail. I was responding to an e-mail I received from Paul when I got word of his death. The shock of his passing hit me hard. I felt in this loss that part of the way God has guided me over the years had ended. Paul's passing threw me off balance emotionally, and for a while I felt lost.

Can You Hear Me Now?

I have been blessed with a few people in my life, like Paul, whom God seems to have graciously chosen to help guide me. Yet, in spite of such friends, there are still times when the voice of God is not very clear to me. I think this has to do mostly with my inability to listen effectively. I allow too many competing voices to drown out the voice of the One who seeks to guide me. More intentional discernment is necessary to help me figure out what is God's voice and what is simply the clamoring of my own ego, self-will, and desires.

As a child I remember going to sleep at night to the voices of my parents and some of their friends in the living room beneath my bedroom. I could always pick my father's voice out from among the group because of its depth and resonance. Even though the walls between us muffled his voice, hearing him comforted me. Discernment is learning to hear God's voice amidst the competing voices so that we may feel assured of his presence and understand his direction for our lives.

Some fortunate folks in the body of Christ have the spiritual gifts of wisdom and discernment. I am not one of them. I have a difficult time sensing direction from God. Most of the time I pray that God would just drop a note in my lap with detailed instructions and a map for following him. If God is more ready to communicate with me than I am to listen, why doesn't God just speak up? What's to be gained by my straining to hear?

One morning years ago at the beginning of a class at Duquesne University, a Catholic institution in Pittsburgh, Pennsylvania, the professor invited us to bow for prayer. I was sitting near a young novitiate working toward her orders as a nun in the church. When the prayer ended she turned to me and said, "You want to know what God's will is for your life don't you?" I was immediately caught off guard by her question. During the silent portion of our prayer time I had actually petitioned God to help me know his will. I was at another crossroads in my life and was struggling to know which way God intended me to go. And so I prayed, "God, speak up! What is your will for me? What do you want me to do?" The young woman obviously had some gift of discernment or wisdom. I answered, "I don't know how to get a handle on God's will for me right now. I'm struggling to know the way." Then she leaned over and said, "Gary, God's will is what your will is." Okay, what does *that* mean? Sensing my confusion she added, "Your heart's desire is to be one with God, right?" I nodded. "And you are doing what you can to nurture your relationship with him. So, isn't it possible that in your journey with God what you will is what God also wills for you?" She went on to explain to me her understanding that God doesn't have one single path in mind for us to follow and so we don't have to stress ourselves out trying to find *it*. Because we are in relationship with God there are many paths we can pursue that will lead us closer to God.

So when we stand at a convergence of paths the question really isn't so much, what is God's will for me? but rather, how will the choice I make strengthen my relationship with God and allow me to be the best *me* I can be? Maybe more than one of the paths we are considering will accomplish this. And so we get to choose the path that most appeals to us *and* honors God.

When You Encounter a Fork in the Road

As I listen for God's direction and try to follow the Spirit's lead, I endeavor to keep in mind that a particular path might be best for me now, but it will not necessarily be best for another stage of my journey. Right now I feel as though I could be doing many different things vocationally to fulfill my calling. Any one of them would allow me to use the gifts and graces God has given me. Any one of them could strengthen my relationship with God. What I am doing right now in ministry is, I believe, the best expression of my gifts, personality style, temperament, and passion for the building of God's kingdom, for doing God's will. But that doesn't mean this will be the best path for me to follow with God for the rest of my life. Before this I was a stewardship consultant and traveled extensively across the country to help churches raise money to support their ministries. I felt called into that work, just as I feel called into this one. When I left pastoral ministry to pursue a career in church consulting, some people criticized me for "switching" from one call to another. They couldn't understand my decision to "abandon" my calling because they understood calling to be static.

At this stage in my life, my sense of calling is much broader, more flexible and open-ended than it was when I became aware of my journey with God more than 30 years ago. I believe my calling is to be about the work of God's kingdom. Through careful discernment I determined that church planting would be the best way for me to fulfill that calling—right now. As God is with us in the journey and our hearts are set on following the Spirit's lead, then whatever pathway we choose will lead us within the broader realm of God's will for us. Our will and God's will are one because we journey together.

When Opportunity Knocks

This year has been an incredible time of transition for my family. We left a church we planted and loved. We moved from a house we had built and transported all our earthly possessions halfway across the country to begin a new life. Our older son was entering the 11th grade and both boys had built many good friendships back in western Pennsylvania. Over a span of 12 years my wife had grown into her own ministry of consulting and leadership training for the denomination that fit her like a glove. She felt she was finally where God wanted her to be. We enjoyed many deep friendships in our church and community. We were living less than four hours away from our extended families and felt secure in the knowledge that we could get to each other quickly in times of emergency. The idea of uprooting ourselves from all of that was heartbreaking at first.

The senior pastor of a large United Methodist Church in central Florida invited me to join his team to help plan and lead their daughter congregation. Members of his church who had relocated to western Pennsylvania and attended the Cornerstone Church I had planted there had recommended me to him.

I was flattered that he would consider me for this opportunity but the implications of such a change seemed overwhelming. I thanked him for considering me but respectfully declined. He was persistent. "Why don't you come here at our expense and look at what we're proposing. I'll show you our target area and then we can visit the beach and just chat." Okay, now he had my attention. I love the beach and thought a free trip to the Florida coast would be great. "It won't be an interview," he said. "Let's consider this a consultation." I agreed.

I arrived at the Orlando airport and made my way to the hotel. My brother, who lives in nearby West Palm Beach, happened to be in the area and invited me to dinner. My brother Rick and I are very close friends and so a chance to spend time with him made this trip even more exciting. The idea of our families living closer to each other was phenomenal.

The next day Bill, the senior pastor, and I spent several hours getting to know each other as we drove through the proposed target area for the new church. As he shared his vision I found myself becoming infected by his excitement.

The remainder of the day we spent basking in the warm sun and cool ocean breeze of Cocoa Beach. Bill and I sat in our beach chairs getting to know each other. At the end of the conversation we both agreed that we would enjoy working together. I confessed to Bill that I was interested but had great concerns about leaving my present ministry and, more important, about the impact a move like this would have on my family. We agreed to discern together where the Spirit might lead us.

That evening we dined with several key leaders of the church. We introduced ourselves and swapped ministry stories. At the end of the meal, the lay leader of the church leaned over and whispered, "I know you're not sure about this but I have a strong sense that God is calling you here." To which I politely replied, "I would appreciate your continued prayers in this."

Tired from the events of the day, I went back to my hotel room. After a brief phone conversation with my wife, I climbed into bed and turned off the lights but couldn't fall asleep. The combination of rich foods, jet lag, and too many conversations kept me awake. Around 3:00 a.m. I surrendered. Turning on the desk lamp I opened my journal and for the next hour began writing out the thoughts that had been swirling around in my head. As I wrote I sensed the Spirit speaking to me in the deepest recesses of my heart, and I jotted down what I thought I was hearing. The page in my journal is marked October 26, and among the scribbled lines in blue ink are these words, "Don't be afraid—I am with you." "You are free to do this." "Use the gifts I have given you." An hour later I cried myself to sleep.

Three hours into a deep sleep the clock alarm not so gently reminded me I had a plane to catch. After navigating the lengthy check-in process that is part of air travel these days, I plopped into my window seat in the very last row. It was a full flight so I knew my six-foot-five-inch frame would be held captive by that tiny space for the next couple of hours. I settled in as best I could.

My mind keep rewinding and playing the events of the past two days. My heart was still in listening mode trying to discern God's voice from among the clamor of airplane sounds, slamming overhead compartments, and the tired announcements from our flight crew.

Once we hit our cruising altitude and everyone settled into the flight, I could sense God speaking again, "I love you. It will be okay. Don't be afraid." I sobbed my way across the Carolinas and along the coast of Virginia. "But what do I tell my wife?" I pleaded in silence. And the words formed in my heart: "Don't worry. I will tell her."

My wife told me later that when I walked into the house that afternoon, she could tell by the look on my face that something significant had happened. Fearing that I might tell her God wanted us to move she said, "I don't want to talk about it now." I remembered what I felt God had said to me—"I will tell her"—and decided not to push her.

Nearly a full two weeks went by before Kim brought up the subject. Waiting that long was agonizing for me. We were walking hand in hand around the neighborhood when she turned to me and said, "I know this has been really difficult for you and I appreciate the space you have given me to process things. I've been praying about this and I don't think it's fair for me to discount whatever opportunity God may be giving you simply because I am afraid. I think I need to go back with you and get a sense of things for myself." I agreed that it would be good for us to do that and reminded Kim that if God was truly behind this I believed he would confirm it for her as well.

The church in Florida made arrangements for us to visit. The pastor worked on an itinerary for Kim that included meetings with potential ministry employers, a realtor, the youth director of the church, and many of the leaders I had met. We were barely through the morning of the first day when Kim turned to me and whispered, "I don't understand it, but I sense God is in this. I think God wants us to come here!"

"What do we do now?" we wondered. "What are the next steps we should take to confirm that God is calling us to this?" We immediately thought of our teenage sons. How on earth were we going to help them catch a vision for this? In our hearts we heard God say, "Don't worry. I will tell them." When we returned home, we shared what we had experienced with them and asked them to think and pray about it for a while. We wanted them to talk with us about their concerns and to hear about some of the good things we felt were waiting for them, and us, in Orlando, including a dynamic youth group, perpetual sunshine, theme parks, perpetual sunshine, beaches, year-round swimming, and perpetual sunshine. The thought of all that seemed appealing to them but the thought of moving away was overwhelming. "Don't worry. I will tell them."

As Kim and I were busy planning our 25th-anniversary cruise, my brother and his family in West Palm Beach offered to watch our guys while we were away. We decided to take them up on that. The boys stayed with their cousins in the perpetual sunshine while we cruised the eastern Caribbean. We had arranged that after the cruise we would pick them up and make a quick overnight trip to Orlando to visit the church, spend time with the youth directors, and attend an evening dinner and service they were having.

Aaron and Jake's eyes widened when we entered the youth room appropriately called the Attic. It's a large room with exposed rafters holding an array of treasures: shopping carts, beach umbrellas, parts of a VW Bug, and even a World War II torpedo. The youth directors met us there and, after bantering with the boys a bit, described the kinds of things the youth of the church were involved in. God was beginning to tell them.

We found our places at the table set for us. Each table had a host family from the church responsible for greeting each guest, making sure introductions were made around the table, and ensuring the food from the kitchen arrived according to schedule. Fortunately for our boys, our host family had two beautiful blond daughters roughly the ages of our sons. As they were seated, I could see my oldest son's eyes widen. All through dinner these four young folks kept checking each other out, smiling profusely, and working to impress each other. When the meal ended, we walked with the crowd from the gymnasium where the dinner was held to the sanctuary for communion. Leaning toward us Aaron whispered, "I think I'm going to like it here! I already know someone." And God told them. There were still many challenges the four of us had to face as we stepped boldly to follow God's lead, but the confirmations we received along the way made the trip so much easier.

Discernment

While everything up till now could be considered discernment, our family felt we needed a more formal process to help us through the conversations and decisions we needed to make. We didn't want the decision we made to be driven by excitement, fear, or compulsion. We wanted to slow things down and meander with God as we gathered the information we needed to make a faith-filled response. While many parts of our discernment process overlapped or unfolded simultaneously, we discovered several specific ingredients were crucial. These included listening, waiting, reflecting, and acting. All of which led to a response of awe.

Listening

When seeking the Spirit's lead as we meander with God, placing ourselves in a listening posture is important. This aspect of discernment is the foundation of all the others. Because the ways Kim and I meander with God are different, for this discernment to be effective we also needed to accommodate our divergent styles of listening.

Kim found reading, taking long quiet walks, and processing things with a close friend to be useful listening tools. For me, writing things out in a journal is like speaking them, so as I reread them I can "hear" what I am thinking. I also tend to process things out loud, so it was important for me that Kim and I had lots of conversation. I tried to read Scripture every day and spend time in silent reflection.

As we listened for the Spirit's lead, we grappled with very specific questions:

- Is what we are being asked to do consistent with what we know about God's desire for us?
- Is this calling consistent with what we know of God's character? God's love?

- Does this opportunity support our Christian principles and values?
- Will following this pathway harm or help others, especially those we love?
- What is our heart telling us?
- Does this fit us—our gifts, graces, and passions for ministry?

Part of the way I listened for the answers to these questions was to take the standard psychological exams that are mandatory for anyone receiving an appointment to a local church. The Florida Conference also required that I take all the church planter's assessments, spiritual gifts inventories, and a variety of other inventories. They too were listening for God's direction.

Another important way we listen to God is through the network of people in our lives whom we trust to direct us. One of my professors and mentors from seminary, Jerry Flora, used to talk about this network as a Circle of Trust. This circle for me intentionally includes people serving in these differing roles:

- A close friend who knows me and loves me no matter what
- A person who is or has been my mentor
- Someone I am mentoring
- A critic
- A counselor
- A superior, which for me is my district superintendent and bishop

When trying to discern and follow the Spirit's lead we can turn to the people in our own Circle of Trust, give them as much information as we can, ask them to be in prayer for us, and then invite them to share insights they have gained from their own unique perspectives.

As I tried to be attentive to the Spirit's leading in this opportunity to come to central Florida, I met with each member of my Circle of Trust, in person or by phone, and shared information, trying not to taint it with my own emotions or passion. Because they live in various parts of the country, this took some time.

One by one the people in my Circle of Trust returned with an affirmation of God's call to go to central Florida. Without exception I was receiving a green light. The final conversation was perhaps the most important, however. Kim and I scheduled a meeting with my district superintendent and bishop. We honestly thought the green light would turn red in this meeting. We enjoyed a good relationship with these leaders, and on many occasions they had affirmed the effectiveness of our ministries. "Surely they will want us to stay and will offer reasons for our doing so," we agreed before our meeting. When we entered his office, our bishop invited us to sit at his table with the district superintendent. Before we had a chance to speak, he confessed to knowing about this opportunity for several weeks. "Since hearing about this, I have been in prayer for you," he said. "I know what a difficult decision this must be for you both." We nodded our heads in agreement. "I know the church and the pastor in Florida. I'm aware of the new church they are trying to plant. I also know that you have the gifts, graces, and passion to do this work. And as much as I hate the thought of losing you both, I believe this is God's will." There it was—the final green light. We talked about the implications of this for the ministries we were currently serving and then joined hands to pray. We agreed that we would continue praying about this for two more weeks, and I would call them with our final decision.

Waiting

The Scriptures tell us to wait upon the Lord, to place ourselves in a posture where we don't press too hard or too quickly for answers or direction. Waiting has to do with delaying making a decision until it is absolutely necessary to do so. We should take as much time as possible so that we can continue seeking God's guidance.

Waiting is a difficult thing for me to do. I like to gather information and make a decision as soon as possible so I can get on to the next thing. But to shortcut the process of waiting is to risk making decisions that might lead us down the wrong path. I encourage people to find out how much time they have before they need to render a decision and then take all of that time to wait on the Lord. Time is always on our side.

Reflecting

Kim and I reviewed everything we had "heard" from God. We discussed compensation, housing, job descriptions, and other employment issues with the church. We discussed our exit strategies with our current ministries and made arrangements to hand off our work to others. We combed through the entire process looking for things we might have missed. We then took a long vacation to reflect on everything and let it settle within us before the next step in the process.

Acting

Finally, after listening, waiting, and reflecting, Kim and I had reached the penultimate step: we needed to make a decision and then act on it. Confident we had spent sufficient time seeking God's guidance and not discerning anything that said we should decline the offer, we made our decision to move to Florida, believing it was the right path for us.

Sometimes I have acted on what I believed was the right path only to meet a closed door. I have sometimes tried to break the door down or force my way inside, but in my experience that never works. A closed door for me typically means I need to step back and do some more listening and reflecting.

I believe that if after all we had heard and experienced in the three-month process of discernment we had chosen to stay, it would have been a mistake. *But* I also believe in the love and grace of God enough to know that God would have continued on the journey with us and blessed our lives, because we would still be about building God's kingdom. Again, we have the confidence we are in God's will not because of what we *do* but because of who we *are*.

Awe

This journey of meandering with God culminated in a deep sense of awe in our knowing that God had been present with us. Even a year later we step back from it all and are grateful for the opportunity we have to be serving God in this place. And while this new church-planting process seems more difficult than the last, we again have the assurance that God continues to be with us.

Unless God Is with Us

No matter which path we choose to follow on our meandering way, even when we are convinced after careful discernment we are clear which is the right one for us, the trip will be a lot less fulfilling and purposeful if God is not invited to journey alongside us.

Going back to the exodus story—God continued to lead the Israelites from their captivity in Egypt toward the promised land in what turned out to be a meandering journey through the wilderness. And they took some pretty serious missteps along the way.

In one of those missteps we find Moses busy conferring with God on the mountaintop. He has left Aaron in charge of the people while he is away. After what may have been days and even weeks without Moses, the people surmise he is not coming back. They track down Aaron and, playing on his own doubts about Moses's return, plead with him to take charge. "Come," they say, "make gods for us, who shall go before us; as for this Moses, the man who brought us up out of the land of Egypt, we do not know what has become of him" (Ex. 32:1).

Stepping in to play the part of Moses in this drama, Aaron collects all sorts of gold jewelry from the people and melts, molds, and shapes it into a calf-god. The people rejoice. Caught up in the adulation of the crowd, Aaron builds an altar to this replacement god and extends a warm invitation for everyone to attend the coronation of their golden leader to take place the very next day.

Sunlight had barely blanketed the valley when the sounds of celebration ascended the mountaintop. Shouts of praise mingling with blackened smoke rising from burnt offerings lift skyward.

God catches wind of this revelry and tells Moses to get back to the people as quickly as possible. But it is too late. The damage has already been done. Filled with anger, God decides to destroy all the people and create a brand new nation out of his servant Moses. But like any good leader, Moses pleads on his people's behalf. God decides to spare them but decides not to travel alongside them (Ex. 33:3).

Feeling lost and, I think, somewhat alone, Moses pours his heart out to God. "You have said, 'I know you by name, and you have also found favor in my sight.' Now, if I have found favor in your sight, show me your ways, so that I may know you and find favor in your sight" (Ex. 33:12–1). How often has that been my prayer to God: "Lay it out for me, God. Show me the way step by step. I need a map, a diagram, anything to help me in this journey. Show me the seminar I should attend, what book to read, what formula to follow and I'll do exactly what you tell me to do."

Check out God's response, "My presence will go with *you*, and I will give *you* rest"—that is, everything will be fine for *you*. (v. 14, italics added). Moses responds, "If your presence will not go, do not carry *us* up from here" (v. 15, italics added). It isn't enough for Moses that God promises to go with *him*. He wants the deal to include *everyone* in his community of faith. God consents to Moses's request.

Unless our ultimate goal is for God to be with us in the journey, no amount of discernment of direction will be sufficient. We need God to be present no matter where the journey leads us.

There are days when the way doesn't seem so clear and when God seems very far away from us. We may struggle in this darkness for a while, which is not necessarily a bad thing. When

God seems distant, I find myself seeking him all the more. It is as Augustine said: "You [God] made us for yourself, and our heart is restless until it find rest in you."[1] The restlessness we sense inside us may be a sign that our hearts are seeking God, that we are yearning for his presence with us.

Counterintuitive though this truth might seem, however, when we feel driven to take the straight course toward our intended destination, even when that destination is alongside our loving God, we might inadvertently fight against the Spirit's leading. Life's interruptions and the side trips they sometimes bring us—even painful ones—are like the zigzags of a ship tacking into the wind and may become the needed opportunities for the Spirit to move us in directions we could not anticipate. So what may appear to be nothing more than a painful crisis may in fact prove to be the gateway to a destination filled with possibilities for new life. When my life is guided by the internal compass of the Spirit rather than driven by the clock, I will experience a new pace in life, a journey from heartache to hope, and a greater sense of companionship with the Divine.

The heart of the meandering way ultimately comes down to this for me: Will I trust God? Will I trust God enough to guide me in life? Will I trust God enough to find me when I am lost? To bring me all I need when I need it? To guide me along my journey of faith, even when the path grows faint?

It stands to reason that if I desire to be in relationship with God and follow the path that most leads me into his presence, then I will want to do whatever it takes to listen to the voice of God's Spirit guiding me. Slowing down the pace of my life, I will lean forward with hands cupped behind my ears and strain, if necessary, to hear God's often still, small voice whispering my name.

Questions for Reflection

1. Have you ever been lost? How did you feel? How did you become "found" again?

2. What is the most difficult decision you ever had to make?
3. What does the statement "Your will and God's will are one because you journey together" evoke in you?
4. How would you describe your calling(s)? When was the last time you felt called by God?
5. What is your personal process for discernment? What components do you think you would like to add?
6. If you have your own Circle of Trust, even informally, who is in it? If not, what can you do to develop one?
7. What do you need from God to take the next step in your meandering journey of faith?

3

Get a Life!

As I am working to slow my pace and be more intentional about listening for God's voice, these words keep bubbling up in the depths of my heart: "Gary, get a life!" My life has been on autopilot for so long, I still find it difficult at times to relinquish control to anyone else, including the Spirit. *I* want to map out the course. *I* want to be in control. *I* want to get there my way and in my time. To be honest, I do pretty well making deadlines, meeting people's expectations, moving from point A to point B with expedience, and generally just taking care of business. As a driver, I have managed to accomplish a great deal. But what I have found is this: in my drivenness to finish one thing and get on to the next, I rarely take time to savor the moment, to enjoy any of my accomplishments along the way. I almost never express gratitude for the part God played in theses successes. And when people compliment me for the things I have done, I dodge their generosity with a response like, "Thanks, but I could have done better if I'd had more time," or something equally unappreciative.

I have come to the conclusion that the only way I am going to truly get a life—a less hectic, frantic-paced, adrenaline-induced rush from one task to the next—is to learn how to live following the Spirit's lead.

I was invited to be the commencement speaker at a university in central Florida. The students in this program took evening and weekend classes for two to three years in order to finish their bachelor's and master's degrees. The majority of them did this while working full time. Most of these graduates had spouses and children who came to celebrate the completion of this exciting chapter in their lives. There were tears of joy and shouts of praise as the students received their diplomas. Before the commencement service, held at a nearby Catholic church, one of the students shared how much she was looking forward to graduation. Weary of the driven pace she had been keeping for two years—working, reading, writing papers, attending classes, and taking care of two teenage daughters—she was looking forward to meandering a bit more, to slowing her pace, taking a day off each week, spending more time with her family, and in her own words, "getting a life." Having been there myself, I could understand.

In my address to these students and their families, I challenged them to think about the bigger picture of their lives. Life is more expansive than the cubicles we inhabit from nine to five. Success in life shouldn't be defined by the number of checkmarks we place alongside our list of things to do. And life must not be held captive by our frenzied quest for more—more money, more prestige, more house, more stuff. The vision we have of life should lift our heads from the merely mundane and raise our sights to consider the lessons life delivers in things that are otherwise hidden from us: the tenacity of the dandelion pushing through the crack of a sidewalk heartens us to endure in tough times; the red-tailed hawk gliding effortlessly on the wind encourages us to trust the breeze of God's Spirit that gently, and not so gently sometimes, seeks to move us out of complacency. With wide-eyed wonder a child studying the movement of a bug reminds us just how marvelous and magical all of life is in its simplest forms. Why is it as children we wish our lives away in the anticipation of adulthood? Then as adults we wish our children away so we can find the time to play again. And when we are old we wonder how we got to the end of our days so quickly and, unless we learned to get a life somewhere along the way, end up mourning the life we could have had.

I still struggle with the battle raging within me between my bent toward drivenness and the desire to meander more in life. I feel as though I still slip between the surface of an insanely packed schedule and the unrelenting demands of those I as a pastor am called to love and lead. This struggle is not what I want to experience; nonetheless I find myself entangled in these competing directions all too often. Then in a moment of graced clarity, when I dare to lift my eyes above the merely mundane, I am reminded that it doesn't have to be this way. I *can* find another way to live. I *can* choose, with the Spirit's help, to drive less and meander more. I *can* color outside the lines and even make some new lines if I like. *I* get to choose. *I* can decide to live my life in a less chaotic way. No one else gets to make this choice for me. I can get a life!

Meeting Ourselves for the Very First Time

I love what I do as a pastor. I can't tell my heart to stop being compassionate. I can't stop being concerned for the poor or those in need. I can't read Scripture without thinking about ways to communicate with others the truths I find. And I don't really want to. This is all part of what I love about following Christ and being a pastor. *But* I don't want being a pastor to totally define me. This is not all I am or ever hope to be. As I write this, I can feel my heart stirring, reminding me that there are parts of myself that rarely get to come out and play. I neglect these aspects of my life because of my drivenness.

For starters there is the artist in me craving opportunities for expression. His desires are too often crowded out by work. There is the disorganized, free-spirited me who really wants to just kick back and take the day as it comes. He gets scheduled out of view. There is the rebellious me who wants to sit with my brother, Rick, and smoke a good cigar. On the rare occasion he does, he often feels guilty about it. There is the fisherman in me waiting impatiently to stand chest deep in a cold mountain stream. After a while he puts his rod and reel back on the shelf in the garage, where it collects dust. There is the lover me who wants to passionately embrace my wife or simply spend an evening snuggling on the couch without being interrupted by the cell phone, doorbell, or (worse yet) the endless cycle of problem solving that fills my head. These parts of me are not *more* important than being a good pastor, but they are *just* as important. They too are part of the wonderfully unique person God created me to be. Without them I am out of balance. To get a life means to get and stay in touch with all of me.

About 20 years into parish ministry I hit a wall—hard. I had been working diligently all these years to be a good pastor. In my pursuit of excellence, I ended up overextending myself so I felt I could never take a day off, vacation for more than a week, or spend more than one night at home with my family without fearing that my work would suffer because of it. The church *did* grow, and our programs *did* flourish. I, on the other hand, did not. I was sick a lot with sinus and stomach problems. My wife and young sons felt like they were in my way most of the time. I did not enjoy life. I felt like a prisoner of the church. I found myself going through the motions of ministry with no real sense of passion or joy. I felt like I was suffocating.

I had connected enough dots in my career to be appointed to the staff of one of the largest churches of our conference. I was a so-called success, and the price of this was exhaustion, cynicism, and loneliness. I found myself wondering if I could ever do anything else besides pastoral ministry. I had been at this all my adult life. It was all I ever known. Maybe it was all I could or would ever do. I felt trapped.

I remember coming home one night from a seemingly end-less string of church meetings and declaring to my wife, "I am not doing this for the rest of my life!" But where else could I go? What else could I do? I could stay where I was but the thought of that was terrifying. I could go somewhere else and do some-thing else, but what? I was trained to be a pastor. Not much of a market for trained theologians and church practitioners out there in the "real" world.

In the midst of this, our church hired a stewardship company to lead us through a building program. I was assigned to be one of the core leaders from the church to work with our consultant. I spent hours with him as he built and led small teams of people to accomplish specific goals in the campaign. After several meetings I found myself thinking, "I could do this. I would love to do this." One evening I stayed around until the last person left one of our campaign meetings. I asked the consultant if he had time to visit with me. I probed him with a series of questions about the work he was doing, the company he served, and the pros and cons of travel. When he was finished answering my questions, he said, "We're hiring right now and, from my observations of you, I think you would be perfectly suited for work like this. What would you think about joining our team?" My heart raced at the thought of an opportunity like that. We decided to meet again during his next visit and talk about it some more.

I was offered a job with this consulting group. I seized it as an opportunity to get out from under the crushing load ministry had become for me. I thought switching to a new job would cure my drivenness and help me meander more in life. I was promised more time with my family. I was told my schedule on the road would be Monday through Thursday with long weekends off and no ministry responsibilities. Sounded great. And it probably could have worked that way had there not been one common link between pastoral ministry and my new work—*me*. Someone once said, "Wherever you go . . . there you are." As I packed my bags to attend the two-week training for my new job, I inadvertently packed my drivenness. With this new job the scenery was different. The work was different. The salary was different (better!). But I was pretty much the same. I remember thinking about pastoral ministry, "Thank God that's over." I never intended to be a parish pastor again. For the first time in a long time, I felt as though I could breathe again. Changing jobs did give me more space for a while. But that space began to shrink as I took on more and more responsibility with the company. In less than six months, I was invited to join the team assigned to design new programs. I was soon training new consultants, which added more work to my already busy schedule. Four days on the road turned into five, then six, and soon seven. I was suffocating again.

One of the challenges of the new work was the cross-country travel; I sometimes landed in as many as three cities a day. Air travel was a real pain at times. Like most road warriors, I learned to feign attentiveness to the flight attendants as they went through their preflight spiel. One of my favorite parts is the description of what happens in the event of a loss of cabin pressure. A mask that looks a whole lot like a margarine tub attached to the kind of skinny air tube you might find in a fish tank drops down from the ceiling and is to be strapped to one's head by an elastic band. Then comes the instruction, "If you are traveling with small children, put your own oxygen mask on first, and *then* help them with theirs." Sometimes an attendant would add, "If you have more than one child traveling with you, put the mask first on the child you love the most." Funny stuff.

But the airlines' principle is useful: for us to be truly fruitful in our work and to avoid the hyperventilation that comes with drivenness, we have to remember to breathe. Just the other day another staff member and I were griping about how busy our ministries had become and lamenting that there seemed to be no end in sight. As we walked together to our next meeting—the third one that day—I jokingly barked out the word *breathe* to the cadence of our steps down the hall, "Breathe, two, three, four..." I know that I have to take care of myself as I am attempting to care for others. I have to put my own spiritual oxygen mask on first. In other words, I need to be doing the kinds of things that will help bring balance in my life, like painting, hanging out with friends, and fishing—the kinds of things that enable my spirit to breathe. But knowing this and doing it are two different things. Few of us know how to find this balance, and the resulting stress that mounts upon us can become an unbearable load. We have to create the space we need to breathe again.

Less Is More

I am a drummer—not a great drummer by any means, but good enough to get by. Early on my drum instructor, sensing my impatience and drivenness (it really is difficult to hide these traits), would say to me, "Gary, a good drummer knows that 'less is more.'" There are some great parallels between drumming and life. There is a tendency when you are first learning to play the drums to want to fill every space with noise. Novice percussionists thought the test of a good drummer was how fast and loudly they could play the song "Wipe Out." Good drummers know the value of rests, avoiding the temptation to fill every space with noise.

One recent Christmas I was recruited to play a drum part for a song our church bell choir would be playing at two of the Disney resort hotels. It had been quite a while since I had had to read music and actually play what was written. Most of the time when I play drums with our praise band, I just play what I hear, which suits me fine. But when playing with a team of twenty other people and following the lead of an accomplished director, I had to play what was written. As I practiced this song on a drum pad at home, I found the most difficult thing for me to remember was the value of the rests. I felt like I should be doing something, even during those intentional spaces. But once I played my part with the choir, the reason for the rests become apparent. In those spaces, other things are happening. A single bell plays its note, ringing out with crystal clarity. Or silence emerges for just a second, suspending the notes before it in midair. These rests can be beautiful things. As in music, so in life—less is more.

I have attended more conferences about excellence and effective leadership than I can count. I also served on a team in our annual conference to discuss clergy excellence in the local church. One year we designed and led an event intended to encourage dialogue among clergy and lay leaders about the issues of clergy effectiveness. Throughout the day comments were made about the importance of clergy participation in continuing education experiences to strengthen their weaknesses, to become better administrators in the church, and to ensure our congregations maintain an outward focus in their ministries. It is hard to argue with the importance of these things. What troubles me in events like this is the implication that our struggling churches would be healthier (too often meaning more people in the seats and dollars in the plate) *if* pastors worked harder, preached better, and became more effective leaders. In other words, if they got busy playing more notes or connecting more dots. I don't recall many of the workshops I have attended teaching pastors the importance of rest—not laziness or irresponsibility but taking better care of themselves, rounding out their lives by pursuing interests outside of the church, taking a sabbath day, or spending more time with their spouses and children. Neglecting these things can leave us feeling breathless.

Learning to Say No

Part of getting a life and breathing better is learning the value and power of one simple word: NO. Many of the pastors and congregational leaders I know have an overdeveloped sense of responsibility for the churches they serve. Wanting their ministries to succeed, they will initiate just about any program, lead any kind of study, and generally do just about anything to make success possible. Feeling indispensable, they will insert themselves in every activity, sit on numerous committees, attempt to provide all the pastoral care—inadvertently filling every space in their already busy lives with more stuff. It is their own version of "Wipe Out," and in time, they may do just that.

A pastor friend of mine described his leadership role in the church as akin to that of a ship's captain. He confessed that he works way too many hours, leads things he shouldn't be leading, and has become somewhat captive to the church because, in his own words, "If this ship runs aground, it is *my* fault. *I* am responsible for the growth and health of my congregation." I love this pastor. He takes his leadership role in the church seriously. He wants to do his very best for the kingdom of God. And I care enough about him to challenge him on his sense of overresponsibility in the church. During a phone conversation I said, "If you're at the helm and someone in the engine room does something to stop the ship or run it aground, how are you responsible for that?" He replied, "I shouldn't have had the person serving at that post *or* I should have trained them better."

The difficulty with my friend's line of reasoning is that we leaders cannot possibly train everyone to do their job perfectly or watch over everyone else's shoulders as they make each move. We cannot be everywhere at once. We cannot stop other people from being human, from making mistakes. We can't even stop ourselves from that.

To fall into the trap of believing we are an indispensable leader in the life of the church, or any organization, for that matter, means to take on more responsibility than we should. We come to believe we can never say no. We must always be available. We will never fully entrust others to do their jobs or recognize failure—when it comes—as opportunity rather than disaster. We will never create and protect the healthy boundaries we need to get a life beyond what we do for a living.

Perhaps you have heard the story about the delivery truck driver making his rounds delivering pets? At every stoplight, the driver would get out of the cab, walk around the truck, and bang on the sides with a two by four. He would get back in the truck, and when he came to the next traffic light, he would do it again. He did this through several stoplights until finally the guy who had been driving behind him this whole time, overcome by curiosity, got out of his car and asked the driver what he was doing. The driver replied, "Buddy, I've got two tons of canaries in this truck. But since it's only a one-ton truck, I have to keep half of them in the air at all times."

I can relate to that. Too often I catch myself still trying to do it all, be it all, and survive it all. I have got the equivalent of a ton of my own canaries in the air, and I am trying hard not to let them all come crashing down around me. Like many wise people before me, I need to remember that I was created by God to be a human being, *not* a human doing.

In his book *First Things First,* author Stephen R. Covey asks, "How many people on their deathbed wish they'd spent more time at the office?"[1] The reality is my inbox, and yours, will never be completely empty before we die. There will always be unfinished tasks, unopened mail, unfulfilled hopes and dreams. Before he was gunned down outside his home, John Lennon is reported to have written, "Life is just what happens to you while you're busy making other plans."[2] If life for us is only about accomplishing tasks, succeeding at work, getting the next promotion, or focusing on what comes next, we may miss the very life we are seeking—one that has space for breathing and as such is open to the more serendipitous experiences of God and others.

If I am going to get the life I really want, one filled with meaningful rests, I need to lighten my load. For me this has to include saying no to some good things so that I have space for the better things in my life, like my relationships with God, those who love me, *and* myself. I think this last relationship is at times the hardest for us. I even feel a little guilty writing about it just now, because I have bought into the notion that I must come last. But what good am I to God or, for that matter, to others if I do not learn the importance of caring for me?

As a professional in ministry, I was taught how to care for the needs of others. Seminary classes in pastoral ministry, counseling, and clinical pastoral education helped to hone my skills for this work. As a trained caregiver, I know how to care for the needs of others. But who cares for me? When we ministers and leaders of the church are hurting, who comes to extend healing and hope? Who cares for the caregiver?

A good friend of mine, Jim, recently completed his first year of ministry in a local church. He had arranged to meet with his worship leader to discuss some conflict they were experiencing in their worship planning. When my friend arrived at this meeting, he was met by nearly a dozen members of the church. The worship leader had invited other members of the congregation, most of whom were not involved in the worship ministry, to join him in confronting Jim on a variety of issues. Jim had been blindsided by this clandestine meeting. After suffering through a barrage of accusations for more than an hour, Jim returned home devastated and demoralized. He spent a restless night questioning his call to ministry. When Jim and I spoke that next day during our weekly telephone meeting, I could hear the pain in his voice. We talked for more than an hour and prayed together. By the end of our conversation, I think Jim felt supported by me and encouraged in his next steps. He shared with me that he hoped someone from that meeting, perhaps a silent supporter, would call him to see how he was doing. Unfortunately that call never came.

As a leader, Jim knows that he needs to teach his people what it means to be a caring community. He has resigned himself to the fact that for now care will be extended mostly one way—from him to his congregation. That's unfortunate, but all too often true of the church. Congregational leaders, laity as well as pastors, are left to tend their own wounds. Because of the never-ending demands placed upon us and the limited amount of time we feel we have to get our work done, we deprive ourselves of the care we so desperately need. We can easily begin to feel victimized by the very work to which we have been called. Sailing in this desert of our own personal pain, we need to learn how to care for ourselves.

Jesus, Our Role Model for Spiritual Health

Jesus was an incredibly busy man. It is hard to imagine anyone with a plate fuller than his. As an itinerant preacher, he traveled city to city to share the good news that the kingdom of God was near. He healed the sick, raised the dead, taught the crowds, debated the religious leaders, dined with people on the fringes of society, and mentored 12 disciples. Jesus worked hard but not to the detriment of his own spiritual well-being. When he needed distance from the crowds who mobbed him for healing and teaching, Jesus withdrew to more isolated places to be alone with God. He sought spaces of quiet and solitude to refresh his soul. In this regard especially, Jesus was a powerful role model for the disciples. They saw the intimacy he had with God. They overheard his soulful prayers. They saw him hungry, tired, fearful, and feeling alone. In these ways they saw in Jesus what it meant to be truly human.

Out of his own human experience, Jesus offered an invitation to anyone feeling unduly burdened by life's load. Matthew records in his Gospel these words of Jesus, "Come to me, all you that are weary and are carrying heavy burdens, and I will give you rest. Take my yoke upon you, and learn from me; for I am gentle and humble in heart, and you will find rest for your souls. For my yoke is easy, and my burden is light" (11:28–30). This invitation extends to every person who is willing to listen. The life to which Jesus invites us sounds to me like the meandering way.

Come

When we are weary and have reached the end of ourselves, what we need is probably not better time management or a course in stress reduction or another church-growth seminar. What we need is not something else to *do* but a life in which we meander to *be* with Jesus.

When we are feeling empty inside, the world tells us to *do* more. But how can any of us do more? Open your calendar or day planner, turn on your PDA, and look at all you have planned to do. We have been raised in a culture that teaches us a meaningful life comes through what we *do* and what we *have*. So it stands to reason, according to culture, that if I *do* and *have* more, I will be happier. If I can cram more into my day—add more canaries to my cargo—then I will have a full life. Yeah, but "full" here should really be spelled "fool."

Jesus said that a healthy balanced life is not a matter of *do*; it's a matter of *come*. *"Come to me."* Meandering is about discovering or recovering the spaces and places in life where we can simply come to be with Jesus. Spending unhurried time in prayer and solitude, reading Scripture in a slow and reflective way, taking walks where we acknowledge the simple signs of God's presence in creation enable us to come to the place where we are simply with God.

Take

When we hear Jesus saying, "Take my yoke upon you," we think, "He's got to be kidding. I'm already feeling driven, weary, and burdened by a thousand different things. Now he wants to add his yoke?"

What is a yoke, anyway? Believe me, I am not a farm boy. The closest I have come to that way of life was when I served two rural parishes. Some of the farmers of my churches tried to instill a little country in me but with limited success. Attempting to fit in, I tried bailing hay, milking cows, and even inoculating cattle. At the end of the day, I was thanked for trying and encouraged to keep my day job.

I remember asking John, one of the cattle farmers in the church, about this passage from Matthew 11 and particularly about the yoke of which Jesus spoke. John taught me that a yoke is a wooden beam designed to harness two animals together as a team, to lighten the load for each of them. Yokes were custom fitted to the animals that wore them, so they wouldn't unduly chafe the animals' skin. By yoking an older, experienced animal to a younger one, the farmer prevented the younger one from driving too hard and hurting itself. Can you see where this is going?

Jesus was saying, "I want to place my tailor-made yoke upon you. I'll be attached to the other side to help carry your load. We'll pull together, shoulder to shoulder." The yoke of Jesus is light because we are sharing it with him as we meander together through life.

I think of the yoke as a symbol of partnership. If I am feeling overloaded, it is possible I am not allowing myself to simply be present with God. I may be trying to bear it all, do it all, or drive it all by myself. I have found over the years that every time I allow my driven life to keep me from spending time with Jesus, my stress level goes up and I feel out of balance. But when I regularly meander a while with him in prayer, worship, recreation, study, and rest, my sense of burden is lifted, and I feel more centered.

Learn

By continually coming to Jesus and allowing myself to be yoked to him, I am learning to trust him more with my life. This means following the Spirit's lead. This continues to be a struggle for a driver like me because, quite frankly, I like to be in control. But when I am yoked with Christ through habitual times of prayer, solitude, and journaling, I feel as though we are moving together in the same direction and at the same pace. As I grow in my relationship with Christ, I am much more willing to allow him to set the direction and the pace of my life. I will want to practice certain spiritual disciplines that open me more to his presence and help me learn to be more of the person God created me to be—a meanderer.

The Value of Spiritual Direction

One of the ways we can come, take, and learn from Jesus as we meander along the journey of life is by availing ourselves of someone who is specifically called and trained to provide what is known as spiritual direction. The practice of spiritual direction has been passed on to us mainly through the Catholic branch of our Christian family. While at Duquesne University, I spent a number of years studying spiritual formation, direction, and counseling. There I learned what spiritual direction is in the classical sense and the value of inviting someone called and trained in this particular ministry to be a part of my spiritual self-care.

A spiritual director is someone we invite to come alongside us as a guide and an encourager in our journey with God. Spiritual directors (or guides) differ from counselors or therapists in that they focus mainly on what a person needs to deepen his or her intimacy with God and to fulfill God's will in that person's life.

When I entered the program in spiritual formation and counseling at Duquesne, I considered myself a fairly disciplined person. I prayed every day for at least an hour. I read Scripture and wrote in my journal. And I regularly fasted from one meal each week. Yet in spite of my disciplined life, I felt extremely distanced from God. I was going through the "right" spiritual motions, I thought, but deep inside I felt devoid of any real sense of joy and peace. When I first met with Carolyn, my spiritual director, she spent some time getting to know me and listening to my story. In our second meeting, she asked me to describe my spiritual life. I presented my laundry list of spiritual disciplines and explained that in spite of doing all these things, I felt like I was in a spiritual desert. God seemed very far away. Carolyn listened intently to me and at the end of our session offered this simple direction. "For the next month I want you to stop doing all those things and instead spend 15 minutes each day in silence. Don't do anything, read anything, say anything, or think anything. Just listen." Easier said than done.

Sitting in silence I became aware of and deafened by the competing voices within me. Silence can be a painfully loud experience. Even when we succeed in shutting out the exterior noise of our lives—traffic, children, telephones—we are bombarded by all the noise inside us. I didn't like what I was hearing. I wanted to do something, read something, think something that would push the voices back into the interior recesses of my heart. My spiritual director knew that I needed to hear and acknowledge these voices in order to distinguish them from the voice of the Spirit quietly speaking within.

In time, and with her gentle guidance, I gradually learned ways to help silence the inner voices of my mind and heart, so that I could be more aware of God's presence. Daily journaling, when I wrote out the longings of my heart as a prayer to God, was particularly helpful because it allowed me to hear myself. Silent prayer, when I would focus on my breathing and allow any thought or image that came to me to pass by like a tree branch in the river, calmed my frenzied mind considerably. Reading brief passages of Scripture slowly and repetitively until a word or phrase seemed to jump out at me helped me to contemplate God's word for my life in that moment, pushing other voices aside.

Even now silence, solitude, and journaling have become like spiritual air for me. I find myself drawn to them regularly, not because I feel like I have to do these things but simply because they help my soul to breathe and keep me open to the abiding presence of God. I would do well to remember that the point of my living is not getting somewhere as fast as I can but being with Someone who loves me and has my best interests in mind.

Getting a Life through Effective Self-Care

I know I am not a disembodied spirit roaming the earth. I cannot compartmentalize the different aspects of myself in neat little boxes marked spiritual, physical, and emotional. I don't have a spiritual self that only comes out of its box on Sunday mornings. Nor do I have a physical self that I keep locked away when praying or an emotional self I check at the door before entering the boardroom or seminar. These three facets of myself are intertwined and inseparable from each other.

At this juncture in my life the most difficult part of getting and staying physically fit is being committed to the healthy practices of exercise, rest, and diet. As I write this I am about 20 pounds overweight, am borderline hypertensive, and take daily medication for high cholesterol and acid reflux disease. Some of this I have inherited from my family of origin, while others are the direct result of poor eating habits and lack of exercise.

Caring for myself physically is an important part of self-care. The apostle Paul wrote in his first letter to the Christians in Corinth, "Do you not know that your body is a temple of the Holy Spirit within you, which you have from God, and that you are not your own? For you were bought with a price; therefore glorify God in your body" (1 Cor. 6:19–20). If my body is the temple of the Lord, then some remodeling is definitely in order.

I am not alone in my struggle with physical discipline. When I am with my clergy colleagues, I hear similar stories of frustration. Too many of us self-medicate with the wrong kinds of food and drink to ease the stress and strain of ministry. We eat too much, work too late, sleep too little, and exercise too infrequently.

I can find almost all kinds of excuses for this self-abuse. I don't walk outside because here in central Florida the weather is way too hot and humid. But I don't exercise inside my air-conditioned house either, even though I have an elliptical machine and a set of weights, because the repetitive motion and static scenery is just way too boring. I keep telling myself that when I can afford to join a gym I will work on this, but I know without discipline it will never happen.

This is a serious stewardship matter for me. As a person of faith, I acknowledge that I own nothing and am really just a manager of God's stuff. This includes my body. How I take care of myself physically has to do with self-respect and my faithfulness to this life God has given me. If I want to meander with God for a long time (on this planet), then I need to take care of myself.

A particularly challenging thing for me right now is the practice of getting out of bed 30 minutes earlier than usual at least three times a week to stretch and take a brisk walk. Coupled with reducing my intake of sugar and fats, this might help me to shed a few pounds and bring my blood pressure closer to normal levels. I know the benefits of a strategy like this. I know I can find the time.

Even as I need to devote attention to my spiritual development and eat, rest, and take care of my physical self, I need also to pay attention to my emotional self. Researchers agree that we have potentially hundreds of emotions, and debate continues over what our primary emotions might be. In his book *Emotional Intelligence*, Daniel Goleman, former Harvard professor and former editor at *Psychology Today*, defines our primary emotions as anger, sadness, fear, enjoyment, love, surprise, disgust, and shame. Goleman suggests our secondary emotions, such as jealousy, hope, and courage, are blends of these primary emotions.[3] Most of us acknowledge the need to care for ourselves spiritually and physically but often fail to recognize the need to care for ourselves emotionally.

When I was serving three small churches in the rustic and impoverished communities of north-central Pennsylvania, I was unprepared emotionally for the demands ministry there would have on me. I was the only pastor in the entire southern part of the county. My parish extended nearly 50 square miles. When an unchurched person died, I was called upon to do the funeral; I had an average of 27 funerals each year. When a family experienced the trauma of murder or suicide—a far too common occurrence in this area—I was asked to care for them. During this period I was physically in the best shape of my life. I was thriving spiritually through my daily disciplines of prayer, fasting, and journaling. But emotionally I was dying inside. Many of these crises called for more of me than I knew I had to give. I felt ill equipped to deal with grieving parents trying to find some sense in their teenager's suicide or the young single mother suffering the loss of her stillborn son or the anonymous death threats we received in the middle of the night or having a gun pointed at me by a drug-crazed man. The fear, frustration, and incompetence I felt was overwhelming.

I remember sitting at the dinner table one evening and right in the middle of our meal suddenly bursting into tears. I cried so hard I couldn't catch my breath. My wife didn't know what to do, and neither did I. I knew I needed help. But where do you go for help when you are the helper? To whom do you turn for counseling when you are the counselor?

I was already a student at Duquesne University when I experienced this frightening breakdown. As a student I fortunately had access to free counseling. It took me a while to muster up the courage to call and make an appointment, but eventually I did. I met with the counselor every week for six weeks. Acknowledging that I needed help learning how to cope with the emotional challenges I was experiencing was enough for me then.

Through these formal counseling sessions I learned the value of making more time for me through miniretreats from stress. The town where I lived was nestled like a dusty bowl between two beautiful hills. I found a crooked trail behind a house across the street that gave me passage to the top of one of these hills. Once or twice a week I would pack a lunch and hike up the trail to the only flat, grassy place I could find. On a clear day from that vantage point, I could count six mountain ranges. I would eat lunch, read some of the psalms aloud, spill my heart out to God, and then lie down for a short nap. Leaving behind whatever stress I had carried with me, I would head back down into the valley refreshed and better equipped to meet the next challenge.

There were some magnificent mountain streams in that county as well. My favorite was about a mile away from my home. I bought an old split-bamboo fly-fishing rod at a yard sale one day for 10 bucks and then visited Perry's Sporting Goods to find out what to do with it. Paul Perry, the owner, outfitted my rod with a reel and line and led me out back to teach me how to cast. I still find myself repeating the words whenever I cast my fly rod, "ten o'clock...two o'clock...ten o'clock," the forward and backward positions of the rod during a cast. I made it a habit to go fly-fishing after most of the funerals I had. Because there was no place to park my car on the side of the narrow road, I would ride my bicycle until I found a place to enter the stream. People got a kick out of seeing their pastor peddling down the road on a bicycle laden with waders and a fly rod. I would spend an hour or two sloshing through the cold mountain stream, focusing only on the tiny fly at the end of my line. To this day I find fishing to be the most relaxing activity of all for me, because as I focus all my attention on trying to catch a fish, I forget about everything else. I never brought a lot of fish home from that particular stream, but I managed to leave a lot of other things there, like anxiety, sadness, and fear.

Most of us have things we can do to emotionally detach ourselves from the cares of this life. These activities can create sacred spaces where we rediscover a true sense of ourselves and God. Reading, walking, fishing, golfing, mowing the lawn, or cooking—these experiences can boost our emotional health, which increases our spiritual and physical vitality as well.

If I am going to get a life that leads me further away from my drivenness, I have to take responsibility for myself and learn how to live differently. I have to create more space in my life by learning to say no to many good things for the sake of a few things that are better for me. I must follow the Spirit's lead by becoming more attuned to God's guidance. My part in this process is to take better care of myself—body, mind, and soul.

The price I will pay for neglecting to get a life like this is that I won't have time for the artist to paint, the fisherman to fish, the lover to woo and snuggle his wife, and the trekker to take a walk with God. In my drivenness I might be able to get a lot done, but the end result will be a two-dimensional life devoid of any real joy. Who on earth wants to live like that?

Questions for Reflection

1. What parts of yourself do you feel you most neglect? What do you need to do to get in touch with them?
2. How is your breathing these days? What kinds of things can you do (or cease doing) to help you breathe more deeply?
3. What are some good things you need to say no to in order to say yes to some better things for your life?
4. What does Jesus's invitation to "come, take, and learn" evoke in you?
5. Would meeting with a spiritual director be helpful in your journey right now? If so, what will you do to pursue this?

6. How well are you taking caring of yourself? What one thing can you begin to do differently to experience better self-care?

4

Keeping Life Real

I yearn in my meandering journey to get a life and keep it real. I want to continue growing into the authentic person I desire to be—a balanced, playful, faithful follower of the Spirit. So I try to give up my drivenness and to follow the Spirit's lead through careful discernment. I discipline myself to do the things needed to foster good health and a continued openness to God. The difficulty for me, as for other leaders, is my life is on public display. I often feel like I am living in a house of mirrors that reflects back the distorted images and expectations others have of me. I know there is more to me than what others see, but sometimes I just can't seem to look past these images, so I develop a rather distorted picture of myself. The crux of the problem isn't so much that I get caught up in the illusions others have of me but that I then create and believe my own false images of self. So I continue to search for the real me, and sometimes what I discover isn't all that flattering.

So far, this is what I have found. I know I have a nasty temper that has led me into a lot of sin. And just when I think I have mastered this unwelcome version of myself, I will get in an argument with my son, the high school senior, and—boom!—it's World War III. Out of anger, I say something stupid that pushes him farther away from me—the exact opposite of what I want to happen between us. Recovering from the resulting silence usually takes us a day or two. Then we will talk: I will admit

I am an idiot; he will readily agree. We will hug and claim a ceasefire. But he and I both know the angry me is lurking just around a corner somewhere. I really wish I could get rid of this part of myself.

I am also selfish. Just when I think I am getting better about putting the needs of my wife above my own, I will go and do something stupid like buy the lawn edger I have always wanted, forgetting that we have been delaying any nonessential purchases so that she can get the new eyeglasses she needs. And worse yet, I will try to be funny about it: "Just think, hon, when you get those new glasses, you'll be able to see better when you're edging the sidewalks." I think I have already told you that I am not very bright.

You see, I know the truth about me. I know at times I am a very impatient and pushy person. I know I crave getting my own way, being in the spotlight, and appearing smarter than I really am. I want people to think well of me. I have worried all my life that if the veil guarding my inmost self was suddenly torn in two and what lies deep within suddenly was exposed to the light, people would point, laugh, and walk away. I want to be seen as someone who has it all together; someone who is smart, funny, faithful, and worth following. What if people could see the other parts of me? The broken, messy, and fearful pieces of myself? They would see a much more authentic me, a kind of Gary mosaic, but would they like what they see?

As I have been talking to God lately, I have been confessing to him, "God, I feel at times like I am one messed-up human being. I still marvel that you called me, of all people, into your service. Even more, I am dumbfounded that you not only love but like me—the Gary who is broken, fearful, foolish, and not really all that bright sometimes—loved and liked by you exactly as I am. You part the veil that guards my heart, look into the depth of my very being, and pronounce me 'enough,' just as I am, to be your friend." This revelation of God's image of me is as true as all the less desirable things I have learned about myself. And when I accept this for myself, I am truly honoring the God who created me.

In Search of Authenticity

My getting a life and keeping it real matters not only to God but also to the people I live with and I serve in and through the church. As a leader of the church, my struggle with personal authenticity has tremendous implications for the church. Many of the failings of the church today have to do with inauthentic leadership.

I have shaped the church by my leadership, and I continue to be shaped by the church. It has affected the person I am—both good and bad. I can't entirely blame the church for the ways I am not authentic. No, the responsibility for that is on me. The church must bear some responsibility, however, for the ways it has been inauthentic and distorted the image of the God who created it. It doesn't surprise me that the church oftentimes strays from what God intended it to be. After all, it is made up of sinful people just like me.

Keeping the Church Real

Over the nearly five decades of my life, the church has been my spiritual anchor and guide. The church taught me the stories of my faith, shaped how I understood myself and the world around me, and opened my heart to the Divine. For these gifts I am greatly indebted. There is nothing on earth like the church, and I am convinced that it is of God. How else could you explain the endurance of the church in spite of our attempts over time to destroy it through greed, bigotry, injustice, and just plain human selfishness and sin?

After investing a lifetime of service as a pastor, I realize how often my heart has been broken by the institutional church. As I was busy planting Cornerstone Church, a district superintendent, who himself had tried unsuccessfully to start a new church, warned me, "Gary, whenever the Spirit begins to fan a flame of something exciting, like the start of a new church, a thousand church people seem to come out of nowhere to beat it out with brooms." Three months after that conversation—after we already had well over a hundred people attending the new church—I was summoned by another superintendent to meet with the senior pastors of three of the largest United Methodist churches of our area. The purpose of the meeting, I would soon discover, was to find a way to put an end to the new church. Each pastor chimed in with their concerns about our growth, our connection to the larger church, and, finally, with my age. "Don't you know you're too old to be doing something like this?" I was stunned into silence by the attempts to extinguish the fire God had fanned in my heart. Not once had I ever entertained the thought that someone 41 years of age was too old for this kind of ministry. I left that meeting more determined than ever to see this through.

As much as I love the church and remain committed to its growth and well-being, I find myself increasingly frustrated with what I see as the church's preoccupation with itself. There are way too many churched people with brooms in hand waiting to beat out any flicker of change, any spark of creativity, any ember of vitality, any flame of truly authentic presence in the world, because creativity and change threaten the status quo and require people to think differently about what it means to be the church in this present age. There's a pointed joke about the church that goes like this: "How many church members does it take to change a light bulb? Change? Why my grandmother gave that light bulb to the church more than 50 years ago!"

Many leaders in the church find it extremely difficult and frustrating to guide their congregations toward becoming a more authentic presence in the world. Having lost a sense of Jesus's call for us to be light and salt, many congregations have become driven more by maintenance than mission. Dwindling worship attendance and financial giving turn these churches inward in an attempt to preserve themselves. Many congregational leaders who feel stuck in situations like this settle into becoming chaplains to their dying congregations or, worse yet, social directors hired to keep the members happy, well-fed, and blissfully entertained. Early in my ministry, I served churches like this. After repeated, failed attempts to help them refocus, I found it best to love and care for them while I worked really, really hard to keep the experience from tainting the image I had of myself and the church universal.

A Worldwide Struggle to Be Real

I recently returned from a two-week cultural immersion in Belfast, Northern Ireland. The church I serve has a 10-year partner relationship with a Methodist church situated on the peace line of Belfast. How strange to refer to 20- and 30-foot walls capped with twisted barbed wire as "peace" lines.

I wasn't there to study the church per se. I was there simply to be supportive of our partners and gain insights into their work toward reconciliation among the segregated Catholic and Protestant communities in Belfast. In Northern Ireland the terms *Catholic* and *Protestant* are as much political designations as anything.

With few exceptions, the churches in Northern Ireland are very small with ever-dwindling worship attendance. I was told that less than 20 percent of the country's population consider themselves an active part of the church, and this was substantiated through dozens of conversations I had with people who claimed a vital relationship with God and yet had no connection with a local church. Their judgment is that the church is at best benign and at the very least responsible for many of the evils of their society. In many people's minds, the church has fueled the hatred and mistrust between Catholics and Protestants or sat idly by doing nothing to promote peace between these groups.

During the second night of our visit, a Catholic school just a block away from our hotel was firebombed. Four of us ventured down to the site of the fire. We watched in horror as the kids hurled rocks and bricks at the police. Though at least 20 yards from the police, they hit their targets. Their stony missiles bounced off the hood and windshield of the police car with a resounding metallic thud. "Why are you doing that?" I asked a group of boys. "It's what we do!" the youngest replied. "Why aren't the police doing anything?" I continued to quiz them. A boy who looked to be about eight years old blurted out, "'Cause they know if they get out of their car, we will kill them." Something in his voice told me he wasn't kidding. Soon older youth and young adults started arriving with cell phones pinned to their heads. We had been warned beforehand by our partners that paramilitary groups send representatives into such skirmishes to assess the situation and make the call, using their cell phones, to either squelch the violence by sending everyone home or fuel it with additional supporters. This event, they determined, was not worth the effort to retaliate. While "minor" events like this one occur rather frequently, major riots, like the one that erupted in this same area in September 2005, happen less often than they used to. Perhaps some sign of peace?

During our visit I met many people who have turned away from the church because of its preoccupation with itself and resulting disconnect from the very purposes for which it was created by Christ—to be his incarnation in the world extending his love, grace, and peace for all humankind, Catholics and Protestants alike. I also experienced the Spirit among the people of Northern Ireland in many wonderfully surprising ways. In spite of the organized church's failure to be the incarnation of Christ to this historically violent and oppressed country, the Spirit continues to manifest his presence through unconventional means— conversations over a pint in the pubs, gatherings of teens in the streets, beautiful vases of flowers prominently placed in the front windows of homes adjacent to bombed-out buildings. I found that meandering with God in these places created an openness in me that enabled me to experience God's presence in even the most surprising places. With the Spirit's guidance, I can see the church as Christ intended it to be—not boxed in by a building but vibrant and thriving in the people around me, wherever I am.

I witnessed *this* church in a handful of Catholics and Protestants called the Bogside Artists who meet every week in a rundown artist's studio to worship God, pray for peace, and work toward reconciliation. Through art therapy, they work especially with children and youth to help undo some of the suffering inflicted on their culture by the myriad forms of socially accepted violence. When I was there I got to participate in bottle painting. As each member of our team chose a bottle and held it before us, we were reminded how the bottle symbolizes violence and aggression in Northern Ireland. The bottle, easily transformed into a "petrol bomb," has sadly been the weapon of choice among many children and youth. We were invited to paint our bottles any way we wanted. The paint and brushes we used made this process intentionally very clumsy and awkward, so that even the best artist among us turned out something simple and childlike. My bottle sits on my desk at work.

I saw *this* church in the handful of "detached" youth workers from an interfaith community group who venture into both Protestant and Catholic communities to meet the groups of youth gathered there on the streets and to build relationships by simply being present with them. There is no God-talk, no religious agenda, just relationship building in its simplest form. After the kids in the streets get to know and trust the youth workers, they are invited to come to a recreation center housed in the Methodist church on the peace line to participate in more structured and supervised activities. The rules there are fairly simple: no drunkenness or abusive behavior is tolerated. Any conversation about God is initiated by the youth themselves.

I saw *this* church in the gathering of women who meet in a support group each week to deal with the spousal abuse that runs rampant in their culture. God is present in the mutual sharing of pain and the offer of unconditional love and acceptance.

I saw *this* church in Father Jerry, who is the head priest of one of the larger Catholic churches of Belfast. Through a program he initiated called Unity Pilgrimages, members of his parish worship in Protestant churches each week to establish a sense of "kingdom relationship" with them. After several years of this unique approach, members of Protestant congregations regularly worship with Father Jerry's parish. Throughout Northern Belfast, the gains the church is making are coming from nontraditional approaches to ministry.

When congregational leaders like us drop our agendas for self-preservation or dominance within a particular community and are willing to meet others where they are in their journey of faith and then meander beside them, God joins us and meanders there too. What rises from this is a more authentic expression of the church.

Leaders have struggled with understanding their role in the church since Jesus started it. When we lapse into driven attempts to do what we believe is *our* work, we sometimes get in the way of *God's* work. Whether preaching, teaching, visiting, leading meetings, or engaging the community around me, I need to remember that the church is not my institution, not my idea of how God ought to work in the world, not a mechanism through which I gain glory and fame. It isn't mine at all. The church is of God and will be preserved through the end of time because God wills it to be so. As a leader I am a steward, a manager, of God's church. To manage what is God's with integrity and authenticity, I need to remember who I am (a sinner saved by grace) and whose I am (a beloved flesh-and-blood child of God).

I remember the postresurrection story of the disheartened disciples making their way out of Jerusalem and the events culminating in the demise of their rabbi. They were on the road to Emmaus with hearts filled with grief. As they were walking the seven-mile journey and recounting the horrors they had just experienced, Jesus came and joined them, but they didn't recognize him. They attempted to fill this stranger in on the details about what had happened to Jesus. Cleopas, one of the two men, was struck by the ignorance of this stranger. "Are you the only stranger in Jerusalem who does not know the things that have taken place there in these days?" (Luke 24:18). Cleopas continued, "[Jesus] was a prophet mighty in deed and word before God and all the people, and how our chief priests and leaders handed him over to be condemned to death and crucified him"

(vv. 19–20). They invited the stranger to supper, and as they sat down to eat, Jesus picked up their small loaf of bread, broke it, and handed it to them. The eyes of the two men immediately were opened to the very real presence of God. I get the sense Cleopas's take on the situation was that certain religious leaders had not only gotten in the way of God's work—by putting Jesus to death—but in the way of God himself. In spite of their misdirected leadership, God prevailed. Jesus is alive! The church is alive!

Seeing Ourselves in the Mirror

What on earth does any of this have to do with us, with our churches, with our meandering journey with God? Unfortunately, a great deal. Too often in our drivenness as leaders to be right, the best, the biggest, or the most powerful, we inadvertently step on the dignity of others. In our misguided attempts to look great to the world, we make others feel less than what they really are in God's sight. Operating out of fear and self-preservation, we have erected our own walls of judgment and intolerance. Through subtle and sometimes not-so-subtle attempts to manipulate or intimidate others to believe what we believe and behave as we behave, we have thrown up walls behind which we can keep certain people out as well as isolate ourselves from the world. Like many people I met in Northern Ireland, people right around us sense those walls and decide there is no place for them in the church.

Many churches say they are friendly and welcoming of others. My own denomination has spent millions of dollars on ad campaigns touting our congregations' openness to others. But just saying we are open doesn't mean we are. How open are we, really, when we chase single parents from our spaces by making it known that their infants and children disrupt our solemn assemblies? Many of the single parents, especially mothers, I talk to work outside the home and have to place their children in child care throughout the week. They feel guilty about this and want to be with their kids for at least part of the worship service. How open are we when the same church that claims it is welcoming of all people, including those whose sexual orientations are different from the mainstream, then bars the gate when these same folks want to become a more active part of our family? We may tolerate the presence of some of these folks in worship but then turn around and block their efforts to serve as leaders, teach our children, or formally join the church as members. For these failings and more, we need to ask forgiveness and pray for the Spirit to help us reflect to all people, by word and deed, the love and grace we proclaim.

In his book *Blue Like Jazz: Nonreligious Thoughts on Christian Spirituality,* Donald Miller, author and popular speaker on issues related to Christian spirituality, tells many colorful personal stories about living on the campus of Reed College, which he describes as a "godless place known for existential experimentation of all sorts."[1] One of the best stories he tells is about an incident during an annual Renaissance festival called Ren Fayre. Miller describes the event as one big party where people throw caution to the wind and engage in all sorts of rowdy behavior. Miller and some of his Christian buddies hatched a plan for expressing their faith at this fair in an unconventional way. The group of Christians decided to dress like monks and invite other students into makeshift confessional booths to confess their sins. The twist was this—the Christians dressed as monks confessed the sins of the church to the students visiting their booths. The response was remarkable. People who were otherwise antagonistic toward organized religion and toward people of faith listened intently; some were overcome by tears, and most expressed gratitude and forgiveness to their confessors. It was a life changing experience for Miller.

As a church-planting pastor, I often speak with so-called unchurched people. I don't really like the term *unchurched* because it tends to paint people in a less-than-flattering light. The problem is, I haven't found a more suitable term—except for maybe *dechurched,* as many people can point to a time when they were once a part of a church. The conversation I have with these dechurched folks almost always gets around to a story they will share with me about an event or experience that caused them to turn away from organized religion. The spark may have been a conflict with another person in the congregation, disappointment with the pastor, being made to think they were unwelcome in one way or another, or feeling as though they weren't sufficiently cared for by their church community during a personal crisis. My experience is that the longer a person is inactive from their faith community, for whatever reason, the less likely they are to remember the specific event that drove them away. However, they never seem to get over the fact that something or someone disappointed them, and from that point forward their opinion of the church is less than favorable.

While we as congregational leaders don't have all the answers for the dissatisfaction many people have with the church, nor are we necessarily the cause of it, we can do things in our relationships with them to perhaps bring them back, even one step closer, to a faith community. We can, for example, meet them where they are as authentically as possible by dropping the act that we are somehow more faith filled, more holy, more acceptable to God, less prone to sin than they are. We can drop the act that we, because we are "churched," have our spiritual act together more than they do. Sometimes the best thing we can do is apologize to them on behalf of the whole church for the ways they have been hurt intentionally or unintentionally by us and by organized religion. Confessing to them as Donald Miller did that we the churched are imperfect, sinful, and self-indulgent people still loved by a gracious God, forgiven a hundred times a day, and apt to trip over ourselves and others as we try to be an authentic community of faith seems to me to be the right place to begin.

As a congregational leader, I realize that the churches I serve will only be as real as I am. Congregations take their cues from their leaders—clergy and lay alike. My desire to be authentic as a person and as a leader gets short-circuited sometimes because I act out of the expectations others have of me, whether they are consistent or not with who I am and what I have been gifted to do. I have tried over these past 30 years to be a good pastor—and I think most people would say that I have been—but looking back I realize that much of the time my motivation for the things I have done was born out of my desire to please others or to look good in the eyes of my superiors and not because I was being the person God called me to be. No doubt this has sometimes kept me from doing the right things, from saying the tough words, from leading in a way that would be unpopular even though I knew it to be the right thing to do. By trying to become what others—usually church people—wanted me to be, I lost a sense of myself.

Now at this stage of my meandering way, I want to be the real deal. I want to live more authentically as the person God created me to be without as much concern for my spectators. But what does that really look like? I have lived the roles others have desired for me for so long. Have I allowed this attempt to please others to irrevocably define who I am?

A Real Earful

This is a silly story but it typifies my struggle to be real. In my previous church, the one planted in a warehouse in western Pennsylvania, I desperately wanted to do something totally out of character for me, to step out of the role of pastor for a moment and do something that would cause people to say, "Wow! I thought I knew him pretty well, and now he's gone and done something like this?" I had been a leader in the church since the age of 18 and, because of that role, felt I had to be good: clean cut, well dressed, well mannered, nonoffensive, predictable, and bland. This version of myself likely came from having been reared in a fairly conservative middle-class home and partly my experience at a Christian college with very strict rules. Anyway, I had an image in mind of what I believed others expected me to be. I wanted to break out of that image, or at least make a hairline crack in it. I owned a motorcycle. That didn't seem to do it. I would occasionally smoke an expensive cigar and drink beer on the back deck of my house (that's pretty rebellious for a Methodist). But that didn't have much impact, I admit, because I usually did that under the stealth of darkness.

One afternoon I was walking through the local mall shopping for a birthday present for my wife. I passed several kiosks advertising free ear piercing. As you look at my picture on the back of this book, you will see that I am a rather ordinary, middle-aged white guy with the kind of face that looks anything but dangerous. But I wanted to look dangerous. I felt I needed to stage a rebellion against the person I felt I had become—ordinary, safe, dependable, and . . . bland. So I did it. I sat in the booth while the 20-something attendant stapled a stud through my ear. When she asked what kind of work I did and I told her, she responded, "Wow! That must be a pretty cool church you've got going there." I felt immediately vindicated and a little more dangerous. I walked around the mall with a new swagger. Surely everyone could see it. Everyone would notice this middle-aged, white, and dangerous guy coming their way.

I went straight to my wife's office, which just so happened to be at the conference center where my bishop and his staff had their offices. Kim's space was near the rear of the building, so I decided to sneak in through the back door, which just so happened to be as far away from the bishop as possible. I wasn't sure I wanted him to know just yet how dangerous I was. I quietly walked into Kim's office and turned my head to reveal the new me. At first, she didn't believe it was real. During one of our vacations at the beach several years before this, I bought a magnetic earring to wear. When the pressure from the magnets squishing my ear lobe became unbearable, I decided I could become dangerous some other way.

After Kim realized the piercing was real, she told me she liked it and asked if I intended to wear it to church on Sunday. Oh yeah, church. I had forgotten about that. The gal at the mall advised me not to remove the earring for a few weeks until it healed. If I took it out for Sunday, I most likely wouldn't be able to get it back in again. But if I wore it, I might create a scene among the less dangerous types. "Hey, I'm my own person!" I quietly declared. "If someone doesn't like it, that will be their problem, not mine." Such is the ranting of a dangerous man.

I was the first one to arrive at the church on Sunday morning. As others eventually came to help with our set-up, I greeted them, all the while attempting to keep my head turned just enough to hide my earring. It was a kid who noticed it first and announced to anyone within a half mile, "Hey, Pastor Gary has an earring!" Some of the young adults from the room came to see this and immediately began talking about their most recent piercing and how they had been thinking about getting another one. I was cool. Before long, however, one of the older couples of the church came to share their disappointment in me for becoming such a bad role model for the kids of the church. That would be their last Sunday with us. The tipping point for me came when my closest friend in the church immediately voiced his displeasure in my appearance. He too had children at home who might get the "wrong" idea from the leader of his church.

I went home that Sunday and took out the earring. I twirled it between my fingers for a while as a flood of emotions swirled inside me—guilt, anger, and sadness, but mostly anger. "What right does anyone have to tell me what I can and cannot do?" I was reminded by more than one person that morning at church that the Bible says we should not do anything that may cause another to stumble. Boy, do I hate that verse! It has been used against me and others like a club to enforce conformity. Is someone really going to lose salvation because I am wearing an earring? Are people's spiritual lives really that shaky?

Okay, it was just a stupid earring, but it raised a lot of questions for me. Why do I care so deeply about what other people think? Why this fear of rejection? Why this need to conform? Does God care if I wear an earring? Is God really going to think less of me? By giving up so easily, was I giving in to the pettiness of others? And what does that say about me? Is it wrong of me to want to make such a big issue over a little earring? I pinned the earring in my journal, just above my quickly scrawled thoughts about the anger, guilt, and disappointment I was feeling. I know my wanting to wear an earring may appear to some to be hardly worth noting, but in some ways that experience was a defining moment for me. I wanted to see whether, as pastor of a church that said it accepted others as they are, I would be accepted as I am. I learned how easy it is for us to say we are open to others and then act in a way that conveys we are not. I personally felt what others must feel when they are judged or at least treated differently because of the way they look.

Many congregations truly do believe they are open to everyone until someone different comes along making them feel uncomfortable. In one of the churches I served, it was a man named Bob Morris, who was poor. Our church said we wanted to reach the poor in our community until Bob showed up (by my invitation); the members around him cleared a space like he was radioactive. Another church I served was a dying inner-city congregation of mostly white, elderly widow women. A rapid demographic shift in this part of the city due to white flight to the suburbs left this very white church in the midst of a predominately African American community. When the congregation said it wanted to grow, I took the members seriously and went door to door in the area surrounding our church, inviting everyone I met to worship with us—blacks, whites, and a few interracial couples. Some of the African American and racially mixed couples actually took me up on the invitation and came on Sunday morning, only to be told, literally, they were not the "right kind of people for our church." When I speak with gay people in particular, I hear painful stories of how they were once accepted by the church until they disclosed their sexual orientation and were then made to feel unwelcome and unworthy. Prejudice really does wear many faces.

I recently visited a church where, and I kid you not, they had two posters on the wall near the entrance to the sanctuary with pictures of certain clothing styles that were on one poster unacceptable and on the other acceptable to wear. As I walked inside, I was met by another sign that said, "No food or drink beyond this point. This means YOU!" Just beyond that sign was another one that read, "Those who truly honor Christ kneel when they receive Communion." The real kicker was the words printed in their bulletin: "Everyone welcome!" Nobody can make this stuff up.

I meet people all the time—faithful people, smart people, good and decent people—who have walked away from the church because of petty things like this and, unfortunately, not so petty things. They have come up against our barricades—our rules, regulations, dress codes, and expectations of behavior—and have returned home muttering beneath their breath, "I don't belong there. I will never do this again." Their experience of us is anything but real. They see us as stuffy, pretentious, often out of touch with reality, and just plain inauthentic. Unchurched people (as we call them) are smarter than we think. They see through our phoniness. They can smell hypocrisy a mile away.

I have said from the pulpit on numerous occasions that I think the church is one of the only organizations that truly exists for the people who are not members. If I believe this, then why do I expend so much of my time and energy making the members happy? By playing it safe, am I unwittingly helping the church construct barriers that only allow entrance to those whose theology, social behavior, and status match my own?

I believe what the world needs now more than ever are real churches with real leaders, congregations who will drop the act that they have it all together, know all the answers, and never ever have a problem. That they have God figured out, packaged neatly in their own denominational cartons, easily explained on overpriced t-shirts, and painted in black and white without the slightest hint of gray. Is this really the God we seek and want to journey alongside of? Not me. Not anymore.

I want the God of mystery back in my life. I want the God who is bigger than any theological construct or dogma could contain. I want the God whose nature cannot be captured on any garment I might wear. I want the God of vibrant color whose incredible brilliance has yet to be named and placed in a Crayola box. I want the God who loves even pierced, struggling, role-playing pastors like me.

Learning to Lighten Up

Part of what it means for me to keep it real is to learn to take myself less seriously. I used to be a much more laid-back guy—at least that's what my wife tells me. I remember in the earliest days of ministry enjoying myself a whole lot more. Maybe I was too naive to know any better, but I approached ministry with more reckless abandon back then. I guess I expected to fail more because I was young and inexperienced. I used to laugh at myself, and others, much more readily than I do now.

I remember vividly one of the first communion services I presided over. Someone had already placed the bread and chalice on the communion table. They were neatly blanketed by carefully placed white linen cloths. It all looked so nice, I never bothered to check the elements themselves. When it came time for the consecration of the elements, I solemnly lifted the linen cloths, folded them neatly, and laid them aside. Lifting the lovely round loaf in the air, I prayed for God to bless it as Jesus did long ago at his final supper with the disciples. As I proceeded to tear the loaf, I continued with the words, "Jesus broke the bread and gave it to his disciples." But the bread wouldn't budge. It was as hard as a rock. I felt for the groove someone was supposed to cut into the loaf, making it easier to tear in half and, finding none, proceeded to dig my fingernails into the bottom of the bread. While maintaining as much dignity as a red-faced and flustered person could, I turned my back to the congregation and, grasping the bread with both hands, tried to break it over the edge of the table. After I strained for what seemed to be an eternity, the bread finally snapped and promptly disintegrated into a billion little pieces. "Oh crap!" I muttered under my breath. "Now what do I do?" The congregation chuckled politely as the dust settled around me. Still holding an orange-size chunk in my hands, I turned back to the congregation saying, "This is my body broken for you. Do this is remembrance of me." I placed the chunk back on the plate from which it came.

Lifting the chalice in the air, I prayed for God to bless it and held it out to the congregation saying, "This is the cup of the new covenant offered for you and for many for the forgiveness of sin. Do this in remembrance of Christ." I then went to take a sip from the cup (a practice I have carried from my Anglican upbringing), and as I did, I felt a slimy gooey mass slide into my mouth. It was the residue that had collected in the bottle of grape juice leftover from the last communion service nearly three months before. Quickly turning my back to the people—again—I spit the mass back into the cup, wiping its tentacles from my chin. I took a few deep breaths and went on. The people gathered at the railings. I held the bread out for them inviting them to take a piece. It was comical to watch them snap off tiny morsels of bread. I then passed by with the tray of cups. Each person took one, held it to their mouths as though taking a sip, and then quickly deposited the still full cups back into the tray as I passed by again. Each person's eyes met mine as we exchanged a knowing look. It was a horrible experience for which I felt very embarrassed. Looking back on it now, I think it has to be one of the funniest moments in my ministry. Though the congregation didn't see the humor in it right away, a few of us eventually got a chuckle out of it *and* made sure it didn't happen again. And there have been dozens of other near disasters.

Cornerstone Church was still meeting in an elementary school when I was asked to baptize the first baby of our new congregation. The family and I stood on the stage around a deep clay baptismal bowl. Another member of the family aimed a camcorder our direction to record the event. I lifted the matching clay pitcher above me as I waxed eloquent about the practice of infant baptism and the symbolism of water. I said a prayer over the pitcher and tilted my hand to pour the water into the bowl. It didn't take long to realize the pitcher was empty. I had forgotten to fill it. My wife sprang into action. She raced up to the platform, took the pitcher from me, and ran down the hallway to the women's bathroom. I made small talk with the family standing beside me and mentioned there might be a ten-thousand-dollar prize for this video if they sent it in to the producers of America's Funniest Home Videos. I also mentioned something about giving 10 percent of the proceeds to the church. Soon Kim arrived with pitcher in hand. "Now you know where the water we use for baptism comes from!" I joked with the congregation. After praying a blessing over the pitcher, once more we proceeded. After that experience, whenever we had a baptism at Cornerstone Church, someone would usually ask, "Did you remember the water this time or are we going to have another dry baptism?" I have learned over the years that it's not the mistakes you make but how you recover from them that matters most.

In my earliest years of ministry, most of the people I knew and served were excited that a young man (just barely out of high school) had such an interest and passion for ministry. They brushed off my failures to inexperience or youthful enthusiasm. Now that I am older, failure just doesn't seem to be tolerated quite as well—by me or by the people I serve. After all this experience, I should know better, right? But that means risk is to be avoided. Without risk taking, however, don't creativity and passion get lost? And with the avoidance of risk comes the loss of any real experience of joy.

As one who has studied cultural trends and church effectiveness for more than 30 years, I believe that if the church is going to thrive in the 21st century, it needs to step out of its box, color outside the lines, stop playing it so safe, follow the Spirit more, and above all else be characterized by contagious joy.

Yet many people in our society still picture the church as a time machine that warps everyone back to the 1950s with a predictable worship style—somber-looking people all facing forward, droning on in monotone voices, and having little tolerance for expressions of spontaneity or joy. Whether this is the reality or not, it is the impression many people have of the church. When guests visit a church that by its own dying behavior confirms the guests' greatest fears, they are even less likely to try again sometime at that church or somewhere else.

I have come to believe that thriving congregations in this century will ultimately be the ones that focus on becoming authentic faith communities that genuinely care for others, are graceful and unconditionally loving of people from all walks of life, see themselves as living laboratories for discovering new ways of doing ministry, and are characterized by uncommon joy. Such churches are never ever dull! Churches that experience this kind of contagious joy can't help but ooze it out through every pore of their collective being and infect everyone else around them.

Such churches will be led by real risk-taking people who themselves have learned to get a life and keep it real. These are men and women who generously care for others as well as themselves, who have personally experienced and now share with everyone they meet God's unconditional love. These are leaders whose personal lives are characterized by joy.

Following Our Dreams to Become Real Again

The meandering journey we are on is worth the personal struggle it can sometimes bring us. The desire welling up in us to be more than we are right now, to make a difference in this world, to get a life, and to lead a church that is authentic, humble, and, yes, often messy is honestly worth the effort, heartache, and pain it may bring us. If we follow our hearts, the result for us can be great joy.

In his novel *The Alchemist*, Paulo Coelho tells a compelling story about a young boy who is learning to follow his heart. The boy travels through the desert alongside a man who is simply identified as "the alchemist." As they journey the boy engages in a conversation with his heart. He learns that he, like everyone else, has a treasure waiting for him, and the heart's purpose is to encourage him to seek that treasure. But because people become preoccupied with so many other things, they no longer pay attention to their hearts. Only children, who have yet to be so distracted by life, have the ability to hear their hearts in a clear way. The boy learns from the alchemist that because of the pain of going unheard, the heart will eventually stop telling people to follow their dreams. The boy pleads with his heart to never stop speaking to him. Should he begin to wander away from his dream, he wants his heart to sound the alarm and promises that he will hear it and follow.[2]

As we journey along the meandering way, will we hear our heart speaking to us? In the still of the night, in a quiet, contemplative moment, amid the noise and clamor of our drivenness, can we hear its whisper, telling us to follow our dreams? Can we hear it convicting us of a life overly absorbed in busyness? Crying out for attention, does it press us to always be real and sound the alarm when we are not?

Questions for Reflection

1. What are some of the illusions you have bought into about yourself? List a few of them.
2. What words would you use to describe the real you? Make a list of these.
3. What have been some of the positive and negative effects the church has had on your life?
4. How are you helping the church remain real to the world? How might you be hindering this?
5. Recall a seemingly disastrous event in your ministry or work that later turned out to be quite funny. What did you learn about the real you in this?
6. How is your heart speaking to you these days? What can you do or stop doing that will improve your ability to listen?

5

Becoming a
Spirit-Led Leader

Much has been written about leadership these past few years. Visit any major bookstore and you will find hundreds of books on the subject. My personal collection of more than two dozen books spans a 30-year period. But only in the last few years, I am sad to say, have I been trying in vain to find that one definitive work on spiritual leadership that could help me develop a healthier nondriven way to lead.

Like many Christian leaders I know, I did not enter the ordained ministry to run myself ragged in driven attempts to do way too many things. I invested myself in this ministry because I sensed a deep passion and desire to serve God and help others. I truly wanted to make a difference in the world. I wanted to know that what I did had a worthwhile purpose. Maybe you had similar reasons for choosing the work you do. We might refer to this passion and desire as "a calling," but whatever we choose to call it, one day we caught wind of something wonderful and compelling and willingly hoisted our sails to catch what we believed was the Spirit of God blowing upon us and leading us onward. That's how I would describe my calling to ordained ministry some 30-plus years ago.

Driven Leadership Leads to Spiritual Dehydration

For the first several years of my pastoral ministry, passion and purpose carried me forward as I relied on the Spirit to guide me. In my youthful enthusiasm, I almost certainly overromanticized ministry in the local church. I was looking forward to guiding others along their spiritual pathways through my preaching, teaching, and general leadership of the church. But wanting to please others, I began to rely less on the Spirit's power to guide me and began to look more to the innovation of certain "success-ful" programs, leadership models, and megachurches to guide my leadership of the church. I bought into my denomination's corporate models of leadership with their hierarchical flow charts. Through leadership seminars, I learned how to write complicated mission and vision statements. Tapping into the explosive growth of megachurches and the incredible wealth of resources they offered, I became a consumer and purveyor of the latest, greatest, most innovative programs I could import into my congregations. Eager to keep up with the times, I jumped on the bandwagon of blended worship, contemporary worship, and the emerging styles that have come on the scene of late. Knowing the importance of small group ministry, I sought and copied whatever model promised the most success in making disciples. Out of my own misguided desire to lead "right," I latched on to whatever programs touted success in leadership.

In my years of ministry up to and including the church I last planted, I realize how much drivenness had affected my leader-ship. I was driven to succeed. Driven to prove wrong those who said I was too old to plant a church. Driven to prove my ability to assemble and lead a staff that would rocket this church into a large Sunday-morning attendance. Driven to become the leader of the next American megachurch. I was driven to buy land and build a state-of-the-art, postmodern facility on it. I was driven to win over anyone who entered the door of our church. Driven to win the approval of others and God.

I gradually came to realize that I was losing touch with my earlier sense of calling in ministry. The outward signs were there. I could see tangible growth: stronger worship atten- dance, greater finances for ministry, a larger staff, more pro- grams, and even a better salary. But somehow it just never seemed enough for me. I can appreciate now something Jesus once said: "For what will it profit them if they gain the whole world but forfeit their life? Or what will they give in return for their life?" (Matt. 16:26).

Inwardly, I felt I was losing track of my soul—*who* I was called by God to be—and instead was becoming the person others wanted me to be. I was doing things in ministry I felt would please those I served. Like a sailing ship without a rud- der, I felt tossed back and forth by whatever wind and waves others created for me. I was expending myself on the outward appearances of success but inside was feeling bone dry. I was missing the opportunities I used to take to catch the wind of God's Spirit. I was coming to the end of my own dry well and facing a kind of spiritual dehydration.

When you are thirsty enough, you will start looking around for any oasis promising a long, cool drink. Not knowing how to work through this period of spiritual dryness, I began looking around for something else—another ministry position, a job that didn't demand as much of my heart and soul, something that would make me feel full.

A letter John Merritt, senior pastor of CrossWinds Church in Dublin, California, wrote to members captures what I and many others have experienced as leaders on the brink of spiritual parchedness in the local church. John was sensitive enough to know that he needed a break from parish ministry to deal with his own drivenness as a leader and to become rehydrated as a follower of Christ. Merritt writes:

> Longevity in ministry is becoming a lost art. So many debili- tating factors face spiritual leaders these days, all working against endurance in ministry:
>
>> we take ourselves too seriously
>> we create our own pressure

> we think that endless work pleases God
> we preach balance and model imbalance
> we let church growth determine self-worth
> we fail to embrace what God is already doing
> we have no life outside the church
> we confuse emotional issues with spiritual issues
> we have lost the art of play
> we mistreat our physical bodies
> we have no time for quiet contemplation
> we neglect those who matter most
> we have forgotten to dream.[1]

When I read these words I immediately thought of my own spiritually parched life and the energy I expended over the years trying to draw water from a dry well.

In the formative years of the church I planted, I drove myself and others hard. I had vision, direction, and purpose. I could see, taste, and smell where I wanted this church to be. I needed everyone to get on board, to give 110 percent, and to sacrifice as much as I did to make the dream become reality. People were remarkably accepting of this drive. They wanted the church to succeed too. I confess to you now that as a leader I was terribly afraid that if I slowed down or stopped pumping the well so hard, we would immediately dry up and become one of the 70 percent of new churches that don't survive past their third year. I was so emotionally linked to the church that when finances and attendance figures were up, I would be up. When they went down, I was down. I know that many pastors struggle with this kind of fear of failure on some level. It makes little difference whether we are serving a church that is large or small, urban or rural, old or new, traditional or contemporary.

Summer was always an especially horrible time for me. Like most congregations, large numbers of families disappeared for weeks at a time in the summer. I couldn't wait for September so everyone would return, attendance would climb, and I could sleep at night. What an awful way to live. Driven. I knew inside I didn't want to continue down this path. But I had been on this driven journey for so long, I wasn't sure I could change direction. I was about to learn that life has a way of nudging us to make some necessary adjustments along the way. If we are open to the lessons they can teach us, pain and suffering can be helpful guides.

Hitting Rock Bottom

After 20-some years as a leader in the local church, I was about to encounter one of the most draining years of my life. It started in the months prior to my mother's death. Our church had lost its funding for our land purchase and put all building plans on an indefinite hold. We decided to lease and renovate a warehouse space, converting it into a ministry center with seating for worship, offices for staff, and classrooms. We exceeded our costs for the build-out of the space by more than 20 percent, and I believed others were blaming me for this further drain on our already stressed finances. Then a month prior to our move from the elementary school where we had been for three years into our first dedicated facility, one of my key staff members resigned his position. We agreed that the job was a mismatch for him, so he graciously stepped down.

In the next few months, we would lose two more key staff people. Financial support we had expected from outside sources didn't come through. Deep cuts, the kind that only come by downsizing staff, had to be made. Three months into our new facility and we had lost three key staff members. The loss was personally and corporately devastating.

In the midst of our transitions, a few families, including some key leaders and solid givers, decided to pull away. This only heightened a sense of fear in me and concern in the church. First land and building, then staff and key supporters. It seemed that all my hopes and dreams for this church were evaporating right before my eyes. I felt I was losing credibility as a leader. I experienced a kind of leadership drought. Making even the simplest of decisions was difficult.

My devotional life, which up to this point was fairly consistent and with its own bent toward drivenness, ceased. Praying had become extremely difficult because I was angry with myself and mostly with God. How could God allow all these things to happen when I had worked so hard, sacrificed so much, and was so solidly committed to his plan? It simply wasn't fair.

My quiet kind of prayer life, driven though it was, had been replaced with what I now can see were gut-wrenchingly honest, albeit one-sided, conversations with God. I pity anyone who happened to be in earshot of my ranting and raving. I would walk in a clockwise circle around our worship space until I was dizzy. Often with hands flailing and feet stomping, my tear-drenched accusations and pleas for help from God spewed out into the room. Looking back, these were probably some of my most honest and productive prayer times.

What was happening to me? I thought I had read all the right books, studied all the right formulas for fast growth, attended the best seminars, spent thousands of dollars on leadership training, and even led the church through the Purpose-Driven Life campaign. Now we were limping rather than leaping forward. I couldn't help but begin to take this personally. "Maybe the problem was *me!*" I thought. So I became more driven in my prayer life. More driven relationally, thinking people wouldn't leave the church if I were more attentive to them. None of this seemed to work. As I struggled with my own issues of leadership, I found myself entering what would become a long spiral downward into discouragement.

Nothing I had ever read and no seminar I had ever attended prepared me for this kind of personal and professional struggle. "Ministry wasn't supposed to be like this!" I reasoned. "If I am doing the work of God, shouldn't it be easier than this? Where is God in this midst of this heartache I am feeling?" I can't help but think of some of my colleagues in ministry and how they face similar personal pain. It doesn't matter the size of the church we are serving. If we are leading out of drivenness, we will eventually hit the bottom of our own dry wells.

Much of the drivenness I recognize in myself and many of my clergy colleagues I also see in many lay leaders of the church. For example, I put in a 15-hour day yesterday that began with a one-hour drive to attend a six-hour training event for church planters. I drove back from that meeting in time to finish a presentation I was going to make at our church council meeting that evening. When the meeting finally concluded, around 10:00 p.m., I was reviewing my day with one of the lay leaders of the church. "Man, am I tired." I confessed. "I haven't been home since I left the house at 7:00 this morning." The words were just barely out of my mouth when I caught what I had said and added, "But I bet the same was true for you today, wasn't it?" In fact, my friend had left for work an hour earlier than I had, came straight from work to the meeting, and had a 30-minute drive home that night. I was already in bed before he got home.

I need to continually remind myself how busy the laity of the church are. They too struggle with issues of drivenness, burnout, and discouragement in their own careers. Everything they do in the local church is layered on top of their "ordinary" lives. Without allowing the Spirit to renew them regularly, they eventually come to the end of their own dry wells. As a pastor I have watched too many lay leaders in the local church hit that place of spiritual aridity. That many of them were not able to recover without becoming inactive in the local church is unfortunate. As a leader I might have done more to prevent this, but how could I when struggling with my own spiritual wilderness? I felt had nothing to offer them.

As leaders, our inability to recognize how depleted we are physically, emotionally, and spiritually may end up hurting us deeply because we cannot seek the healing necessary for our own well-being. And it may hurt the body of Christ, the church. We need to discover a healthier posture of leadership that begins, first, by seeing and accepting ourselves as we really are—uniquely gifted yet limited children of God on a journey following the Spirit's lead. If we can learn to lead from that place, then we will be less tempted to be driven by our own egotistical need to be spectacular or accomplish great things. And we will be less likely to allow others to squeeze and shape us into whatever kind of leader will best suit their purposes for the church.

Spiritual Leaders Are Made, Not Born

We have probably heard it said of some people, "He or she is a natural-born leader." I don't buy that. My own experience is that leadership is something we grow into. When I entered pastoral ministry, I may have been the designated leader of a local church, but believe me, I was anything but a leader. I wasn't even sure what a leader was or did. Rarely do we step into ministry with everything we need to be effective leaders. Leadership is something we have to work to develop under the Spirit's guidance, and an important part of that process is learning everything we can about ourselves.

Important tools like spiritual gift inventories and personality assessments weren't readily available to most people when I started in ministry. Most of what I learned about leadership came through what my dad would call "the school of hard knocks"—good, old-fashioned trial and error. Certainly there must be a better way.

Our seminaries and Bible colleges do little to prepare clergy to be effective spiritual leaders in the local church. They might train men and women to become theologians, biblical scholars, and caregivers, but without more formal guidance and training in the area of spiritual leadership, our congregational leaders are left to figure too many things out for themselves, such as how to help leadership teams in the church discern the Spirit's leading, how to manage conflict when it arises, how to work toward consensus so that people do not feel violated by voting, how to encourage and support lay leadership so that the church doesn't become overly pastor- or staff-driven, and how to design meetings in such a way that they become opportunities for spiritual formation.

Most pastors and lay leaders want to do their very best. None of us enters ministry because we seek opportunities for failure. We want to get it right, and so lacking formal training in spiritual leadership, when we see good things happening in other places and pastors who appear to be successful in ministry, we want to know what they did to get there. We are so hungry to become effective leaders, we are willing to invest several days or even weeks and sometimes thousands of dollars each year to attend seminars and workshops. We buy the books, promise ourselves to practice the principles, and having picked up a new dance step or two, return home to our churches to begin acting like those we have observed. We might discover that much of what we learned simply doesn't work in the context of our own ministries. But not to give in to complete discouragement, we sign up for the next dance lesson at whatever church seems to know better moves. And so it goes until we find the latest, greatest trend or product promising us personal and corporate success. Or, as the case may be, we move to another church and start the process all over again. Moving from one place of ministry to another may initially alleviate the leadership stress we feel at the time, but without taking the opportunity to learn more about ourselves in the midst of such stress, we may inadvertently delay the important work that needs to be done in our own personal development. This was one of the leadership lessons I had to learn the hard way.

Blooming Where We Are Planted

During my third year as pastor of the Austin Church in north-central Pennsylvania, I faced a leadership crisis that threatened the effectiveness of my ministry there. The church had been experiencing significant numerical and financial growth. New faces entered the sanctuary every week and for the most part were warmly welcomed into the church. However, one woman—the matriarchal leader of the church—was threatened by this growth. I had heard rumors that Lillian had been quietly trying to dissuade people from visiting our church. It was reported to me that she would say things like "You don't want to come to our church, because our pastor is terrible" or "Our church is much too old and formal for younger families like yours." Of course, I didn't believe Lillian could be saying such things. Why wouldn't she want the church—her church—to prosper? That was just ridiculous. Then one Sunday as I was standing in the pulpit ready to begin the service, I heard Lillian speaking loudly to a new family as they entered the back of the church some 30 feet away, "If new people like you keep coming to our church, there won't be enough room for those of us who belong here." I couldn't believe my ears! I stood there in shock for a moment, struggled to gather my wits, and then started the service. Though greatly distracted by even the sight of Lillian that hour, I managed to keep my composure and push through it.

The next morning, before I had a chance to call her, Lillian appeared at my office door. "Pastor, I need you to sign this form recertifying me as a lay speaker in the church for this next year." Lay-speaking status is granted by the United Methodist Church to laity in a local church who have completed continuing education classes on things like preaching, theology, and leadership in the local church. Lay speakers are also required to serve in a leadership capacity in their congregation under the guidance of their pastor. Imagine the timing of Lillian's request.

I asked Lillian to sit down, and as calmly as possible I recounted for her the reasons why I could not and would not sign the form granting her a renewal of her lay-speaking status. I began with a story. "Lillian, if you were to drive by Austin Church one morning and saw someone standing by the foundation of the church swinging a sledgehammer to knock the blocks out from beneath the building, what would you do?" Without hesitation, Lillian straightened in her chair. "Why I would walk right over to them and do whatever it took to stop them." (Lillian was in her late 70s but spry enough to do something like that.) "And if I couldn't stop them, I would find someone who could," she continued. I took a deep breath and prayed for God's guidance as I formulated my response. "Lillian, I witnessed you doing something yesterday morning that was just as hurtful to the church as someone knocking the concrete blocks out from under it."

Lillian and I discussed the things I heard her say to the visiting family that Sunday morning and the rumors others had passed on to me about the things she had been saying out in the community about me and the church. I learned from her that the rumors were true and had been born out of her fear of losing what she had come to love—a small, tight-knit church family. Lillian felt all that she had loved about the church was in jeopardy of being lost to all the new people who were coming. I told Lillian that, as a lay speaker in the local church, she needed to work with me, not against me, in the ministry of the church and that I felt I had no choice but to delay her recertification until the following year. I suggested that Lillian and I meet together on a weekly basis for a month and then once a month after that to work through some of the issues that divided us. To my surprise she immediately agreed to this. We agreed that we would invite another leader in the church to meet with us for the first few sessions so that we would keep on track. We mutually agreed on a man we felt had good conflict-management skills. I felt positive about the direction we were heading. I didn't know that the storm was only just beginning.

As the matriarch of the church, Lillian was related to more than half of the members of that congregation. The next Sunday as I stood in the pulpit to preach, more than 20 people, Lillian's family members, simultaneously rose from their pews. Scattered throughout the congregation, they stood quietly and defiantly for what seemed to be an hour (actually it was only a minute or two), and then, with as much commotion as they could make, they stormed out of the church. For the second week in a row, I was stunned speechless. I waited until the last demonstrator left with a slam of the door and picked up where I had left off in my sermon. Looking back on that event, I have no idea how I managed to keep my wits about me.

Immediately following the service a handful of people met me at the back door and pleaded with me to reconsider signing Lillian's papers. They implored me to go after the people that left, apologize to them, and beg them to come back to the church. I replied to them that I could not do any of those things. I told them about the plan Lillian and I had agreed on, but it was little consolation to them. I stayed with that plan.

As a result of my decision not to sign for Lillian's recertification, our church lost about 20 members. Some of them were Sunday school teachers, leaders of the board, and strong financial contributors. The one person we didn't lose was Lillian. To her credit, she stayed active in the church and met regularly with me. We worked hard together. With the help of the other church leader who guided us, we were able to voice our concerns to each other, discuss our theologies of ministry, and debate our understanding of the meaning and mission of the local church. We sought to ground our dialogue in Scripture by reading and discussing the book of Acts. We continued these conversations over the course of the year, and when the opportunity came for her recertification as a lay speaker in the church, we celebrated the signing of her form over lunch. By the end of my sixth year of ministry at this church, Lillian had become one of my closest friends and ardent supporters—a tribute more to her than to me.

Several days after my confrontation with Lillian, I met with my district superintendent so that he was aware of the struggles I was facing with Lillian and her family. I was fortunate to have a district superintendent (who works with the bishop in ministry appointments) wise enough to leave me in that mess. "I can support your request to the bishop for another ministry appointment if you wish. But I feel you and the church are best served by working through this conflict," he said. I had already indicated to him that I felt it would be best for me to stay, and I did for several more years.

I know at times moving on to another ministry setting is best for us as pastoral leaders. Sometimes working through the conflicts in our ministries is not possible. At times our leadership style is such a mismatch with the particular needs of a local church that it is best that we seek something else. At times, however, the best thing we can do as leaders is to stay where we are and struggle to make things work. My most fruitful experiences in ministry came as the result of working through the tough times. When I remained committed to the local church I was appointed to serve and, more important, to becoming the spiritual leader God desired me to be, I grew as a leader. Spiritual maturation begins when we seek to know ourselves in light of the God who loves us. Truly effective leadership grows from there as we seek to know the people we are called to serve, oftentimes in the midst of chaos.

Getting to Know the Congregations We Lead

When we seek to follow the Spirit's lead toward greater fruitfulness in ministry, we want to learn as much as we can—not only about ourselves but also about the uniqueness of the congregations we are called to serve. As leaders we should discover everything we can about the church's history, its journey of faith, and the unique gifts and graces it has corporately been given by God for effective ministry. Meeting with church families and congregational leaders early on will help us to get a clearer picture of the wonderfully unique congregation we serve. And that picture will only be complete when we study the community in which the church is located.

We often make broad assumptions about our churches and communities, and that is unfortunate. We are fortunate, however, that companies like Percept exist, providing detailed demographic information about every community in the United States. For a reasonable fee, they deliver profiles and analysis about the people around our churches, including a breakdown of age groups and lifestyle information, such as education levels, income averages, ethnic backgrounds, religious preferences, and even the style of worship people might prefer. Someone once said, "If we aim at nothing, we are sure to hit it." To be most effective in ministry, we need to know who it is we are called to serve.

In my mania as a leader, I have at times inadvertently looked beyond the people sitting right in front of me. These folks were important sources of information about their church and community. Many of them had lived through the unfolding chapters of their church's and community's unique histories. Attempting to push things along, make things happen, and drive change—whether anyone (besides me) wanted it or not—I became disconnected from the people in my congregation. This became more apparent to me about 10 years ago, when I was then serving two rural churches in southwestern Pennsylvania, near the West Virginia border.

I served these two churches part time while working on my doctorate at Duquesne University. Each church was well over a hundred years old and completely surrounded by farmland. Locals used to joke about the county's being populated by more cattle and critters than people. Each congregation included families that had lived in the area all of their lives. Some of them were direct descendants of the families that founded the churches. On a "good" Sunday morning, the larger of the two churches, Fairview, would have about 50 people in attendance. Sometimes that number was boosted by a stray dog that would wander in.

Two years prior to my serving these churches, I had been trained by my denomination in conflict management, visioning, and goal setting strategies for the local church. I had used some of these strategies to lead a church I had previously served to significant change and transformation. In a little over a year, that church, in north-central Pennsylvania, grew from 30 mostly older adults to 120 mostly younger persons. I figured what worked in one church setting should work in every congregation. (Did I mention yet that I am a slow learner?)

Six months into my ministry in these two rural churches, I decided to unleash my wealth of knowledge and experience. Certain that both churches would explode with growth, I tinkered with their worship styles, attempting to make them more contemporary, introduced more theologically in-depth Bible studies, and tried to get everyone on board with a novel evangelism program to reach their unchurched neighbors. (I hadn't taken the time to learn that their unchurched neighbors were mostly family who had left the church after some falling out with the pastor or kin). No matter what I tried to do in these churches, little changed. The same faces showed up in worship each week, only one or two people came to my Bible studies, and my innovative evangelism strategy was a big flop. I grew frustrated and disillusioned. Had I invested more time getting to know these congregations and their ministry settings, I could have avoided much of this stress.

I didn't realize the depth of the problem until I shared with a pastor friend, who had experience in church consulting, the frustration I was feeling at these churches for not following my lead. At my request, she came and met with me and several core leaders of each congregation. After an evening of lively dialogue, my friend summed up her explanation of the conflict we were experiencing like this: "You, as pastor, and the lay leaders of your congregations are on the same dance floor; you're just not doing the same dance." As pastor, I was attempting to jitterbug. They were doing something closer to a square dance. And we were stepping all over each other. What we learned around the table that night made perfect sense to us. We ended up having good laugh about the whole thing and affirming our friendship with one another. These were great people.

The issue wasn't that I was a bad leader. I just wasn't in step with them or they with me. That experience opened an important dialogue for us. Each of us determined we had some work to do. After continued conversation, they decided they needed to be a little more open to the new ideas I offered them—like an occasional chorus led by guitar or having a lay person give the children's sermon from time to time. I decided I needed to put aside my desire to transform these churches into something they could not or would not be and invest more time learning about their needs and how I could better serve them as a chaplainlike pastor.

That summer I visited every household in both churches. My only agenda was to hear their stories, to get to know their surroundings, and to pray with them. It was an awesome experience.

By the end of these visits I had gained about 10 pounds from eating their great country cooking, but, more important, I had gained new friends and a level of trust and intimacy I would never have thought possible. We were learning how to dance together, and like every good dance, someone needs to lead and someone needs to follow. In ministry, the roles of leader and follower shift back and forth. Sometimes good leadership means we lead, and sometimes it means we follow. True wisdom is knowing that both are necessary.

Good Leaders Were Once Great Followers

Every good leader begins their journey by following someone else—a parent, a friend, a coach, a colleague, or another role model. My quest to become a spiritual leader would ultimately open me toward understanding the importance of following others. I was 18 years old and looking forward to graduating from high school and moving on to what I thought would be a career in art. In my senior year, I had entered and won a districtwide contest for a four-year scholarship to a rather prestigious school in northern Pennsylvania. It was a dream come true. Only one problem. I was also struggling with a call to the ordained ministry. At the time I wasn't sure what such a call really meant. I only knew I wanted to do something connected with the local church to help people and to serve God. I decided not to take the scholarship in order to pursue some aspect of ministry. The art teacher who had coached me in the process was greatly disappointed in my decision and tried hard to dissuade me from ministry. But the calling I felt compelled me to pursue the path toward ordained ministry.

I shared my sense of this calling with my pastor, who immediately affirmed it and passed my name on to a district superintendent, who that next week called to offer me "a wonderful opportunity." A dying inner-city congregation, Riverside Church in Harrisburg, Pennsylvania, needed a pastor. A photo still hung in the back of the sanctuary depicting a human chain of men, women, youth, and children linked arm in arm and encircling what was the completed first phase of a three-phase building plan. This first phase included a temporary worship space built next to a six-room education wing. Eventually, a large brick sanctuary was to be built above the education wing. The temporary worship space would become a chapel. But the plan would never be fulfilled.

When I arrived for my first Sunday, just three short years after that photo was taken, a small group of 20, mostly elderly, widow women were meeting each week in the temporary sanctuary. (It's a good thing I developed a soft spot for widow women as a young child. That served me well in this church.) The complexion of the neighborhood had changed rather suddenly with the white flight of younger families moving to the suburbs. Multiracial, lower-income families had taken their place. Only the elderly of the church remained, mostly because they had nowhere else to go.

The Christian education wing had not seen a child's face or felt a teen's energy in more than three years. Walking through that facility for the first time and seeing the residue of a once vibrant family church was eerie. In what used to be busy Sunday school rooms, dusty tables sat littered with open boxes of crayons and partially completed pictures of Jesus and the disciples. Yellowed artwork hung sadly by thumbtacks on the walls, as though their young artists would return any moment to claim them.

I entered the ministry with a fairly clean slate. I felt strongly enough about wanting to serve God that I jumped at the chance to pastor this church. I had a great deal to learn about leadership, and school was now in session. I spent four years in this church cutting my ministerial teeth. The district superintendent who appointed me there was right when he said it would be a testing ground for my calling. It was that and more.

I was fortunate that God had long surrounded me with men and women who took me under their wings. Many of them did not know that was what they were doing. Yet sensitive to the Spirit's leading, they came and walked alongside me in my journey toward becoming a leader.

Good Leaders Are Guided Followers

My first real ministry leadership guide was already waiting for me when I was assigned to Riverside Church. I followed a wonderful man and mentor named Rayburn Fritz. Reverend Fritz was retiring from ministry—again. Twice before this he had retired, and both times the bishop asked him to step back into ministry part time to fill in until a suitable pastor could be found. This time his suitable successor was 18 years old and so wet behind the ears he was dripping.

Though officially inactive from ministry, Reverend Fritz was willing to talk with me whenever I needed guidance or a friend. He patiently helped me develop and deliver my very first sermon. He stood several paces behind me at the funeral home when I conducted my first memorial service. He answered my phone calls, even at odd hours, to guide me through whatever challenge I faced. God blessed me richly through this kind and gentle man. And God provided other leaders to guide me along the way.

Sometimes the best guides in life show up uninvited or un-announced. After about three months of preaching every week at Riverside Church, two men took pity on me and decided to help. Ted Sykes was vice president of a local bank and Afton Schadel was an officer in state government. One Sunday morn-ing, Ted and Afton showed up toting video equipment. They set up a camera about halfway down the center aisle where they could get an unobstructed view of their neophyte pastor. See-ing them both standing behind the camera they had aimed at me made me incredibly nervous. I had no idea what they were intending to do. For the next couple of years they videotaped my sermons every week and immediately following worship we would lock ourselves in my office for the review. The first few weeks of this were incredibly embarrassing and painful. By my own admission, I had no idea what I was doing behind the pulpit. Week after week they dissected my preaching. Together we reviewed content, gestures, pacing, eye contact, enunciation, and my propensity to blush anytime I stumbled over a word.

I will never forget the Sunday Ted and Afton shared their motivation behind this: "Gary, we want you to be the best pastor your next church has ever had." Now some folks would have been insulted by a statement like that, but I understood the hearts from which it came. They cared for me enough to lead me and I was honest enough about my weaknesses to follow them.

I don't know about becoming the best pastor my next church ever had, but I do know that I was becoming the best me they ever had. I believe the Spirit led these men to guide me and to help me develop the skills needed for effective communication. I was open enough to the Spirit's leading to trust what these men were doing and follow their direction. I am far from what I want to be, but I am much more comfortable with that knowledge now than I was even five years ago. My personal and professional growth continues, in part, because I still find myself surrounded by great guides. Some of these I sought out and some of them, like Ted and Afton, just showed up one day because they felt called to do so.

I have been richly blessed by guides like Reverend Fritz, Ted Sykes, and Afton Schadel as well as countless others who helped me find my way toward more effective leadership. What I have learned from people like them is that in humility we have to set aside our own inclination to figure things out for ourselves and learn to listen to the direction of the Spirit spoken through others. Whether they knew it or not, these early guides were teaching me to be a follower so that I could someday become a better leader. For this guiding process to be effective for me, I had to adopt a different posture—a more meandering one—that helped me to slow down, listen more for the Spirit's leading, and be patient enough to work through whatever issues or challenges I was experiencing.

As leaders our need to be guided never ends. The people we count on to lead us will be determined by whatever needs we currently have, but more important, where we sense God may be leading. For example, in this particular stage of my journey as a church planter I need the prayerful guidance of other church planting pastors. As a result I am committed to meeting weekly—by phone or in person—with another church-planting pastor. Through this peer coaching, Tim and I share our experiences in ministry, including successes and failures; listen intently to what the Spirit seems to be saying in and through us to each other; and pray for one another's needs. In addition to this relationship, I also have a professional coach working alongside me.

Unlike the guides I have mentioned who have helped me more in my own personal development as a leader, my professional coach offers a more objective, outside perspective on my specific leadership role as a church planter. Though interested in me personally, his main objective is to offer insights into the work of church planting. Jim has reviewed and made recommendations on our search for land; the pace at which we are developing critical components of our emerging ministry, such as small groups and the formal launch team; the marketing and promotion of the new church; and worship development. I have found his insight and experience in church planting to be an invaluable resource for the work I am doing.

I was not always in a position to hire a professional coach like the one I have. Most of the churches I served either did not see the need for such opportunities or felt they could not afford them. Cornerstone, the church I planted in western Pennsylvania, could not find the money in their budget to secure such a guide for me, so I was led to a neighboring pastor, Steve, who graciously agreed to serve in this role. About 10 years before I planted Cornerstone, Steve had planted the church he is serving. He also served as the chair of our conference initiative to plant new congregations. From the beginning Steve was an enthusiastic supporter of my ministry, so it was easy for me to ask him to consider becoming my guide, and he agreed to serve in that role without charging me or the church.

For nearly three years Steve and I met monthly. We would meet early in the morning for breakfast near his church, about 30 miles from mine. I always came to the table with the agenda for our time together. Steve would listen to whatever I wanted to share and then ask questions to further draw me out. His questions and the way he phrased them were meant to help me think out loud and begin to discern the answers to whatever problems or challenges I faced. At times I simply shared my heartaches with Steve. And at other times I met with him to celebrate some of the victories I had gained.

I have learned that working with a guide, whether peer or professional, is an invaluable part of becoming a good leader because it reinforces for us and for the congregations we serve that we do not have the capacity to lead alone and that ministry is meant to be a journey that is shared and supported by others.

In each of these guiding relationships I have had over the years, I can sense the Spirit's leading. Both in conversation and the time of reflection that follows, I am able to set aside my drivenness—even if it's just a brief time—to consider how God is at work in my life. As I articulate my feelings, thoughts, fears, and desires, I find myself slowing down enough to be able to hear myself, and the Spirit, more clearly. In moments of such clarity, I often discover new insights about myself and the issues I am facing as well as a deeper appreciation for how God is at work in my life.

Gaining a sense of direction through guiding relationships helps me to be a better follower. My experience has led me to conclude that, especially as an extrovert, the Spirit leads me best when I am in community with others. Maybe that is why Jesus said, "For where two or three are gathered in my name, I am there among them" (Matt. 18:20). Certainly God is with us when we are alone, but isn't there a greater sense of God's Spirit when we are on the journey with others?

Spirit-Led Leaders Guide Others along the Way

Spiritual leadership is both a guided and a guiding journey. Guiding others can sometimes be a difficult and demanding task. Leading a congregation can at times be like sailing a ship into the wind. We face resistance from within from our own drivenness, fear of failure or rejection, and lack of competence and confidence. And we face resistance from without from a culture that has become skeptical about organized religion, that often views the church as irrelevant, and that is pulled away from the church by a multitude of competing activities. These inner and outer forces of resistance make guiding the church difficult at times. We may feel as though we are trying to sail a ship through the desert. We have all the right equipment on board and our sails are raised fully to the wind, but the resistance of the sand beneath us makes guiding the church seem impossible at times.

When sailing a ship into the wind, a technique called "tacking" is required. Tacking means steering the ship at an angle to allow the wind to fill the sails, which propels the boat forward. To stay on course, the ship must be tacked left and right in a zigzagging pattern. To help navigate the ship, the tallest mast will sometimes have what is called a "telltale" fixed at the top. This telltale is like a miniature weathervane that shifts freely to indicate the direction of the wind. The telltale is especially helpful for novice sailors like me. By watching the telltale, I can easily see which way the wind is blowing and adjust the sail and tiller accordingly. If I head too much into the wind, I won't catch as much of it in the sails, and I am likely to slow down or stop altogether. If I am approaching the wind at too much of an angle, then I am likely to be blown too far off course or, worse yet, tip over. Only by watching the telltale will I know at what angle to steer the ship to maximize its power.

God has given us the Spirit as a kind of internal telltale—a spiritual guidance system. If we are seeking to follow the Spirit's lead, as we strive to make progress against the things that impede fruitful ministry, the Spirit will let us know which way we need to go. If the Spirit is telling us that we are guided too much by our own egos, drivenness, fears of rejection, lack of competence or confidence, and overcommitment, and are therefore moving in the wrong direction, we need to listen to the Spirit's prompting and be willing to tack, or shift our course, and begin living and leading differently.

As those who follow the Spirit's lead, we have a responsibility to help others discern and follow the Spirit's guidance in their own lives. This means we need to see ourselves as guides for those we serve. We need to help others slow the pace of their lives enough to hear the still small voice of God.

When considering this role, we need to remember that the work we do is like sowing seeds in the soil of the human heart. Jesus reminds us of this in one of his parables:

> "The kingdom of God is as if someone would scatter seed on the ground, and would sleep and rise night and day, and the seed would sprout and grow, he does not know how. The earth produces of itself, first the stalk, then the head, then the full grain in the head. But when the grain is ripe, at once he goes in with his sickle, because the harvest has come" (Mark 4:26–29).

The seeds sprouted and grew without the farmers help. Because the church is a living organism, made up of uniquely created people, we as leaders can only do so much by our own power and initiative to organize, shape, or grow it. Perhaps the most effective thing we as leaders can do is to foster the kind of environments where people can more easily receive the seeds of God's love and grace.

Before we sold our home in Pennsylvania in preparation for our move to Orlando, I had to plant some grass in the corner of our back yard. The previous summer we had placed a three-thousand-gallon swimming pool there, and it smothered all the grass beneath it. When we took the pool down, what was left looked like a 15-foot landing pad for a UFO. The people who had recently purchased our house decided grass would look better back there, so I bought some seed along with several bags of fertilized topsoil. I carefully followed the directions on the bag. I watered the landing pad twice a day for a week. Every morning I went out, stooped down, and inspected the earth for signs of "frog hairs." For more than a week nothing appeared. I was tempted to add some more fertilizer to the area, thinking maybe it would force the growth, but a neighbor who knew better (a rather astute guide) encouraged me to be patient. I had to keep the scripture in mind: the seeds grew without the farmers help. I could have added more stuff to the dirt, scattered more seed, and watered it more frequently, but I was told it wouldn't help. I just had to keep the environment healthy and let God do the rest. If I can learn to do that in my backyard, maybe I can learn to do that in my own life and even in the church.

I used to describe the church as a kind of factory where we as leaders receive the raw materials, the unchurched people God sends us, and move them through an intentional process of shaping and molding, so that they come out the other side as disciples of Jesus. It sounds simple enough. It seems to make sense. There's only one problem. People are *not* raw materials we can easily manipulate or maneuver. People who are unchurched come trusting that we will not abuse them. They are hoping that they will be accepted as they are and, with gentle and patient guidance, find their own place of belonging among us. They are looking, I believe, for the space they need to meander with God and for guides who are willing to lead them there. What they are not looking for is someone who will drive them like cattle to places they are not ready to go.

Sara came to Cornerstone Church while we were still worshiping in an elementary school. I noticed how she came in late and left a little early. For several months Sara followed this pattern. I was accustomed to greeting people in the hallway after worship, but Sara always managed to time her departures well so that she would not have to be greeted by me or anyone else.

One day at the conclusion of worship, Sara waited for me at the bottom step of the stage. I was surprised to see her there. She held out her hand and introduced herself. "I'm Sara, and I've been attending here for a couple months now. I sort of believe in a Higher Power but I don't buy into Jesus. You tend to talk a lot about Jesus in your messages, and I know you believe in him and he means something to you personally. I'm not there. I come back each Sunday because I always find something in your messages to help me through the week. I've noticed how friendly your church is, too. I have a question for you. Having said all that, am I still welcome here? Is there a place in your church for a person like me?"

I assured Sara that she was welcome and encouraged her to become as involved as she wanted to be. I told her she would find the space and time she needed to decide on her next steps. I gave her some material about the various ministries of the church and invited her to visit my own small group. And I thanked her for her honesty.

Sara continued coming each week. Eventually, she began to arrive with the rest of the crowd and after worship linger around for coffee and snacks. Soon she brought her boyfriend, Jack. Over the next three years, the two of them became regular attendees of our church and Sara became a regular participant in the small-group meeting in my home.

About four years into her journey with us, Sara came to my office and asked if there was anything I needed someone with administrative skills to do for the church. I suggested we could use help developing more effective ways to welcome and follow up with first-time guests. Remembering her experience as a newcomer in our church, Sara said she would love to help us with this ministry.

As is my practice as a leader, I asked Sara to take a couple of weeks to pray about this opportunity and to meet with one or two others in the church to discern if this was where God was leading her to be. At the end of this discernment period, Sara felt God had indeed called her to this ministry. So she became a member of the hospitality ministry team and, to my surprise and delight, when it came time to elect the team's leader, Sara graciously volunteered.

Over the course of her journey with our church, I had the joy of watching Sara meander into the places she needed to be. When we create the kind of environment where discernment is valued and driving is minimized, people like Sara can grow into the kind of people God intends them to be. The seeds grew without the farmer's help.

Spiritual Leadership Comes from a Heart Centered in God

The letter Pastor John Merritt wrote to his congregation concluded with these words:

> In the middle of leading worship [during a Willow Creek leadership conference] Dieter Zander [a teaching pastor at Willow Creek] quoted a verse which cut right into my heart—"not by might, nor by power, but by my Spirit, says the Lord Almighty" (Zech. 4:6). I experienced a release and re-energizing that is hard to translate on paper. But from that moment on I became less caught up in doing, performing, and serving *for* God and more caught up in being, enjoying, and receiving from God. And in the process, I began to reconnect with my Creator and Lover, who refreshes and restores my soul.[2]

In my own drivenness as a pastor I have often neglected my relationship with God. Having at times been so busy leading others to the well, I have merely taken quick sips rather than the full gulps that I needed to quench my own parched life. I confess this to myself and to God and now desire the spiritual refreshment that is promised to each of us as we abide in the Spirit. I need such refreshment, especially as I am called to lead others.

My visits to the well will continue to include reading some of the good leadership material out there. It will include attending seminars to hear the stories of how other leaders experience God and find fruitfulness within their own ministry context. And it will involve my own meandering with the Spirit alongside the people God has drawn into the community of faith I am part of. With these many companions, I will continue seeking to answer these important leadership questions:

Where is God in this place?

What is God blessing or seeking to bless here?

Where does God seek to lead me in God's own unique ways and in God's own perfect timing?

What are the needs of the people in this congregation? How can I help them find a sense of belonging in this journey of faith?

How can I nurture the kinds of environments where people are called to meander with God at their own pace, in their own space, with the love and encouragement of fellow pilgrims?

As we discover answers to questions like these through a prayerful process of discernment, we will become more open to the Spirit's leading and find the commitment and vitality we need to be spiritually focused followers who then become spiritually centered leaders. A willingness to walk with others as they strive to meander with God is at the heart of spiritual leadership.

Going On

Learning to live—and lead others—at a meandering pace can be downright difficult, especially if you are a driver like me. At times Spirit-led meandering seems a whole lot like trying to sail in the desert. It can be slow going at times. It will severely test our faith and call into question the very purpose of our existence.

I feel a little bit like the apostle Paul when he wrote to the church he planted in Philippi: "I do not consider that I have made it my own; but this one thing I do: forgetting what lies behind and straining forward to what lies ahead" (Phil. 3:13). I confess: I talk a good talk about meandering, but I have a long, long way to go. It really is something I aspire to. I don't want to drive my life like some crazy person hell-bent on getting somewhere as quickly as possible. I don't like the anxious feeling I get in the center of my chest when I am stressed out by all the things I have to accomplish. I am turning fifty in six months, and I really do want to alter the pace of my journey, learn everything I can about myself, be more aware of the awesome presence of God, become more attuned to his voice, be the real deal, laugh at myself a whole lot more, preach from a stool without apology, and lead others with integrity. For now I guess I will just put one foot in front of the other and see where this journey takes me—and try not to be so afraid.

By the way, we just moved into our new home. It has a lovely pool out back. Best of all, even in the deep end, the water doesn't go over my head. And some people say there is no God.

Questions for Reflection

1. When did you first sense God's call upon your life? How was that calling affirmed for you?
2. What kind of dance are you doing in your present ministry setting? Is your dance in step with those you seek to serve?
3. What kind of leadership training have you experienced both formally and informally? What might be your next step in your growth as a leader?
4. Who have been or are now your leadership guides? And whom are you guiding?
5. Who are the "Saras" in your ministry? What are you doing as a leader to help create the space they need for the Spirit to be at work in their lives?

Notes

Chapter 1

1. "Schedule Interrupted: Discovering God's Time Management," *Christianity Today*, February 2006, 43.

Chapter 2

1. *The Confessions of St. Augustine*, trans. E. M. Blaiklock (Nashville: Thomas Nelson, 1983), 15.

Chapter 3

1. Stephen R. Covey, A. Roger Merrill, and Rebecca R. Merrill, *First Things First* (New York: Simon and Schuster, 1994), 17.
2. John Lennon, "Beautiful Boy (Darling Boy)," 1980. *Double Fantasy*, Geffen Records, 33 rpm, EMI.
3. Daniel Goleman, *Emotional Intelligence: Why It Can Matter More Than IQ* (New York: Bantam, 1995), 289.

Chapter 4

1. Donald Miller, *Blue Like Jazz: Nonreligious Thoughts on Christian Spirituality* (Nashville: Nelson Books, 2003), 37.
2. Paulo Coelho, *The Alchemist: A Fable about Following Your Dream* (San Francisco: HarperSanFrancisco, 1988), 131, 132.

Chapter 5

1. Used by permission of John Merritt.
2. Ibid.